THE WISDO~~M~~
INNER GUI~~DEBOOK:~~
THE 64 FACES OF AWAKENING
COMPANION TO THE WISDOM KEEPERS ORACLE DECK

*Gaze into the faces of the **Wisdom Keepers**,
and you will feel seen and supported
with the eyes of Compassion and Love.*

Created by **Rosy Aronson, Ph.D.**

The 64 Faces of Awakening
The Wisdom Keepers Inner Guidebook
Text and Artwork Copyright © 2015 by Rosy Aronson

Seal Pup Press
PO Box 138
Berkeley, CA 94701
sealpuppress.com

ISBN: 978-0-9970230-0-8 first paperback edition: November 2015

Art and writing by Rosy Aronson
Deck design by Kim and Rosy Aronson
Editing, Publishing and Creative Startup Consulting by Ann Cameron
of *AC Creative*
Editorial and Design Consulting by Colette de Gagnier of *Mystic Alchemy Design*
Editing Support by Evelyn and Marilee Aronson

Key words and concepts related to *The Spectrum of Consciousness* by
Richard Rudd's *The Gene Keys*, Gene Keys Publishing © 2009

WisdomKeepers.net
RosyAronson.com
64faces.com
64faces.org

While certain *Wisdom Keepers* may happen to resemble individuals you know, the *Wisdom Keepers* and their stories were created to reflect archetypal essences and transformative themes with no intention of representing specific people, characters, places or events.

Dedicated to
the *Wisdom Keeper* in you...

DRAGONFLY WINGS

dragonfly with organza wings
come closer, let me perceive
the intimation of immortality
embodied in a slender frame
artful shimmered iridescence

low existence on water's edge
burdened wingless, colorless,
tethered to earth, debased
by such a primitive condition
you waited in deep shadows

renewed rising in blissful flight
you travel now in six directions
and view the earth from heights
that once you were oblivious to
dragonfly, you are me, I am you

you bask in summered sunlight
and grace timeless smooth rocks
with such silken, bountiful beauty
dragonfly teach me as I observe
an early morning transformation

~ La Belle Rouge

The Human Face

The infinite, writes her stories
on the contours of the face;
the ultimate reality shining forth
from living mirrors.
The seeker need only cast their gaze
upon this holy countenance.
Lost in open receptivity,
absorbed in living light,
All 'other' disappears as we breathe alone...
Together,
Face to Face
with the mystery.

~ Tanmayo Lawson
www.premtanmayo.com

CONTENTS

IT TAKES A VILLAGE!

My deepest gratitude goes out to all of the friends, family, clients, *Designed to Blossom* participants, and the *Gene Keys* community for all of the ways they've held the vision and supported this labor of love.

I'd like to extend a special thanks to those who played a more central, unique or catalytic role in the birth of the *Wisdom Keepers Oracle Deck*: Richard Rudd, Ann Cameron, Colette de Gagnier-Rettner, Simant and Patty Herkins, William Sebrans, Elijah Parker, Eve Chan, Stephen Wong, Jan Collins, Teresa Collins, Cyndi Silva, Jenny Karns, Rona Renner, Gina Rose, Mark Fromm, Mbali Creazzo, Sreed Vijayarangam, Rebecca Fisk, Prem Tanmayo, Olaf Schäfer, Elitsa Stoichkova, Jessica Hadari, Susan Strasburger, Jan Camp, Joell Jones, Kerane Marie Lomonaco, Valerie, Brendan, Zoe and Ella Creane, Rachel, Owen, Zev and Jacob Walker, Beth, Brian, Elianna and Audrey Washington-Deane, Ruby Arzt, Karin von Daler, Mireya Alejo, Karen Clothier, *Binah Zing, Aunt Sarah, Grandpa Sam, Grandma Jewel, Ra Uru Hu*, my bio-soul sister and creative midwife Marilee, and my wonderful, supportive parents and editors Neil and Evy, my extremely patient, wise-beyond-her-years and FUN daughter Maya, and my beloved 'partner in crime-and-creativity' Kim, without whom this deck (and my sanity) would not exist.

And of course, I give thanks to the spirit of the *Wisdom Keepers* themselves, who have come to me (and to this world) at a time when they are deeply needed.

INTRODUCTION TO
THE WISDOM KEEPERS

These are paradoxical times on our planet; times of great suffering, and times of great promise. More than ever, our survival as a species depends on our ability to honor and respect our differences while acknowledging and embracing our interconnectedness.

My intention in bringing forth these *64 Faces of Awakening* is to reclaim, reflect and celebrate the soul of the world, a miraculous multiplicity of ONE. It is my way of illuminating the incredible uniqueness of the individual person or tribe, as well as engaging in a deep, intimate experience that transcends 'self' and 'other.'

These faces embody the very kind of peace, love and understanding that I long to see in the world and experience in myself. They represent both ancient and new human archetypes that connect us with our collective evolution and indigenous roots. Since many of the *Wisdom Keepers* are elders, one of my deepest intentions for this project is to honor and celebrate the wisdom and radiance of a population that in our youth-obsessed culture all too often go unseen, under-appreciated and under-utilized.

THE HUMAN FACE

Often called the 'organ of emotion,' the human face is a dynamic canvas and one of our most powerful channels of nonverbal communication. From the moment we are born, we are constantly monitoring, mirroring and reading the faces around us, looking for cues, so that we can better understand what others are feeling and assess whether we are loved and safe in the world.

The human capacity to form healthy attachments is deeply determined by the quality of presence in the faces of our early caregivers. Studies have shown that when babies are met with empathic faces, they relax and thrive. When they are met with neutral to 'negative' expressions, they often become emotionally disorganized and struggle to form healthy bonds as they grow.

That said, we are immensely resilient. We have the potential to heal old wounds through the formation of new loving attachments. Just looking into a face that reflects love and acceptance can have a lasting impact on how we see and experience ourselves, as well as on our ability to give and receive love.

The human face also transmits deeper states of consciousness. When we spend a long enough time looking into the eyes of a truly present being, we begin to access our own inner radiance and aliveness.

The *64 Faces of Awakening* have come specifically to recognize your potential, reflect your beauty and receive your love. Connect with each face as you would a friend, a grandmother, a mentor, a lover or a guide. Relax into the gleam in the eye. Allow yourself, over time, to develop a sincere relationship with each of the *Wisdom Keepers*. You will be surprised at the power of their medicine. Though each face is different, they all come to love you unconditionally, to reveal important truths about who you are, and to help you remember the dreams that have been seeded in your soul.

THE CREATIVE PROCESS

The creative process behind the birth of the *64 Faces of Awakening* has been mysterious, whimsical and highly intuitive. Often these beings have emerged through my dreams and imagination. Every once in a while I've felt a strong pull to capture the essence of a person—or a hybrid of people—who have inspired or moved me on an archetypal level. On a couple of occasions, I've seen a person walking down the street or sitting in a cafe whose energy and expression I've felt compelled to bring forth in a drawing. And there have been times when others have shared their visions of a face with me, and I've integrated those visions into an image.

When drawing, I consciously enter into an intimate, meditative and intuitive space. I allow myself to drop in to a highly rhythmic, detailed process—dot by dot, line by line. Slowly I watch the white paper and black ink intertwine and lose themselves in a staccatoed dance... until there is no black, and no white. No this, and no that. Just a multi-faceted being emerging from the background—infused with universal and archetypal symbols, inviting me into hidden worlds and emanating a presence that I can feel in my bones.

The process of creating these faces has been exceedingly soothing to me. It has not only allowed me to work through my own grief about the wounded and conflicted state of the world, but to apply and receive my own form of medicine.

When I gaze into the eyes of these wise beings once they're fully formed, I feel seen, cherished and supported. While at first I might be enamored and awed by the specificity of their beauty, in the end, it doesn't matter what their ethnicity is, or their religion, or the color of their skin. Or even their age. What matters is the possibility of transformation that their gazes inspire.

As I spend time with them, I find myself feeling increasingly relaxed, trusting, patient and forgiving in my everyday life. I feel invited to become more loving, more alive, more empowered and more real.

Ultimately, I see these drawings as soul windows, or medicinal mirrors. Each being is an exquisitely unique reflection of the truth that the face of Love and Compassion is universal, and of the potential that resides deeply within each of us.

BIRTH OF THE STORIES

Just as I had little control over who came through when I was bringing the *Wisdom Keepers* into form, I had little control over what they had to say when it came time to creating the *Oracle Deck*. Writing this *Inner Guidebook* has been a deeply intuitive process that has required complete surrender and trust.

As I allowed the *Wisdom Keepers* to reveal their personal stories to me, the most important thing I learned was that each one of them earned their wisdom and discovered their gifts by not only surviving painful and challenging experiences, but by embracing them, as Jung encourages us to embrace our *Shadows*. I learned that these radiant beings aren't that much different from you and me. They are deeply human. How comforting it is to remember that very few of us get to be present, loving and compassionate in this life without experiencing some kind of pain, loneliness, discomfort and fear! So wherever you find yourself at this moment, if you are learning to greet your challenges with openness and curiosity, you are also very likely on your way to becoming your own keeper of wisdom.

Please note: The *Wisdom Keepers* and their stories have been channeled as a way of reflecting archetypal themes and are not intended to represent specific people.

64

As I intuitively received the *64 Faces of Awakening*, and then their transformative stories, I recognized them as keepers and transmitters of archetypal wisdom. I felt drawn to exploring how they might be connected to other significant archetypal inquiries, such as the work of Carl Jung (with his emphasis on the *Shadow*), the ancient philosophical system of the I Ching (with its 64 hexagrams), and the plethora of modern, mystical and creative manifestations born from the I Ching, including Ra Uru Hu's *Human Design* and Richard Rudd's *The Gene Keys*, two central streams of inspiration in my work with clients and students.

The I-Ching and the number *64* have unusual significance in many areas of human explorations, including art, cosmology, religion and science. I've explored these areas in my personal, spiritual and professional studies over the years. As I've integrated them into my work as a counselor and teacher, they have come to hold special meaning and power for me.

When I explored ways to expand the *64 Faces of Awakening* and bring these wise beings into the hands of people through a practical and empowering *Oracle Deck*, I found myself resonating most strongly with the profound work of Richard Rudd, author of *The Gene Keys*. With care and gratitude, I did my best to incorporate the most essential concepts and key words of *The Gene Keys* into the text in this *Inner Guidebook*, found at the introduction to each *Wisdom Keeper*. My core intention in weaving together the *64 Faces of Awakening* and *The Gene Keys* through this *Oracle Deck* is to explore ways the *Wisdom Keepers* can serve people in a practical, playful, psychologically insightful and personally transformative way.

THE GENE KEYS

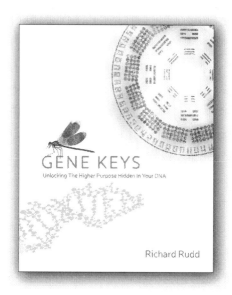

As I've shared, *The Wisdom Keepers Oracle Deck* was in part inspired by the work of Richard Rudd, a teacher of world mythology, an award-winning poet and the author of *The Gene Keys: Unlocking the Higher Purpose Hidden in Your DNA*.

While this oracle deck stands happily on its own, it is also intended to act as a warm welcome into the world of the *Gene Keys*. I highly recommend that anyone who feels drawn to this deck consider exploring *The Gene Keys* book or participating in the growing online *Gene Keys* community. They will greatly enrich your *Wisdom Keeper* experience!

WHAT ARE THE GENE KEYS?

Understanding some essential elements of the *Gene Keys* will facilitate your use of *The Wisdom Keepers Oracle Deck*.

The *Gene Keys* is a body of knowledge aimed to help transform our core self-beliefs, expand our consciousness and release our individual creative genius into the world. There are 64 universal archetypes that lie at the heart of the *Gene Keys*.

The 64 *Gene Keys* correspond to the 64 hexagrams of the I Ching, the 64 codons of our human DNA and the 64 *Wisdom Keepers* in this deck. Each of the *Wisdom Keepers* reflects and transmits the essence of their particular archetype through a unique story. Their stories are here to illuminate how each of the archetypes can play out in our lives and how they transcend culture, ethnicity, race, religion and age.

Weaving together a tapestry of psychology, sociology, mysticism and indigenous understanding, the *Wisdom Keepers* have the power to catalyze a profoundly transformative and mystery-celebrating journey in you.

THE SPECTRUM OF CONSCIOUSNESS

When exploring the *Wisdom Keepers*, you will notice that each *Wisdom Keeper* is connected to three essential concepts, the *Shadow, Gift and Siddhi*, as used by Richard Rudd in the *Gene Keys*. For Rudd, these define a *Spectrum of Consciousness,* and refer to archetypal states that he correlates with the human experiential stages of *Survival, Service and Surrender*. The *Shadow* has its roots in Jungian psychology, while *Siddhi* is a Sanskrit term used in both Buddhist and Hindu mystical traditions.

SHADOW: When we are worried about our survival, and fear is in the driver's seat, we find ourselves in *Shadow* territory. Our *Shadows* can be expressed in repressive or reactive ways.

GIFT: When we are more oriented towards serving others and honoring ourselves, than protecting and defending ourselves, we more naturally share our *Gifts* with others and feel a sense of belonging in the world.

SIDDHI: When we have entered a pure state of expansion and have completely surrendered our sense of separateness into the Whole, we have entered the realm of the *Siddhi*.

Each of these three stages plays an essential role in our psychological and spiritual development as human beings. There is no *Gift* without the *Shadow*, no *Shadow* without the *Siddhi*, no *Siddhi* without the *Gift*. These states of being (or frequencies) breathe and dance together as we evolve.

Understanding how the *Gift*, *Shadow* and *Siddhi* are constantly interacting with each other throughout our lives can help us engage with the *Wisdom Keepers*—and ourselves—with greater compassion and patience. As we awaken to the full spectrum of our human consciousness, we become more gentle with ourselves and we begin to notice larger growth patterns at work.

It is important to understand that even if we've been on a sincere spiritual path for years, we are still likely to find ourselves moving in and out of the *Shadow* and *Gift* states. We may re-experience feeling stuck in familiar ruts, yet this is perfectly natural. Periods of sadness, fear and frustration can actually be quite fertile if we can just hang in there without too much self-judgment. Over time, as we revisit the *Shadow* realms with less resistance, we notice that their grip loosens—they no longer determine our attitudes, decisions and actions.

The feelings and thoughts seem real enough, but we are no longer trapped and controlled by them in the same way. We begin to sense our evolution as our love and desire to serve become bigger motivators than our fear and need to protect or defend ourselves. In our efforts to serve, our unique *Gifts* begin to find their natural expression and we become increasingly available to experience pure states of love, understanding and aliveness.

So, when you read the *Wisdom Keeper* stories and contemplate how their underlying themes may be playing out in your own life, I invite you to hold the *Gift, Shadow* and *Siddhi,* and the delicate interplay of these states, in your heart and mind.

You will notice in this deck that the *Wisdom Keeper* stories focus primarily on the *Shadow* and *Gift* expressions of each archetype. The *Siddhic* realms are communicated energetically in the cards, through the expression in the eyes, the symbols on the face, and the invitation into a sacred relationship.

Each *Wisdom Keeper* has the potential to penetrate deeply into your heart and open you up to a mystical experience. As it always is with the *Siddhi,* there is nothing you need to do, nothing you can make happen. Just stay open, and surrender.

THE SHADOW

To confront a person with his shadow is to show him his own light.
~ Carl Jung

We pay special attention to the *Shadow* to understand how it emerges and how best to work with it in our lives. The *Gene Keys* and the *Wisdom Keepers* teach us how the *Shadow* holds the key to both our personal and collective transformation.

When we are children, most of us learn that if we act or feel one way, we get the love, safety and attention we need; and if we act or feel another, we are met with disapproval, rejection or threat. Because we depend on our parents or primary caretakers for emotional and physical sustenance, we quickly and instinctively learn to reject the parts of ourselves that leave us feeling unsafe or insecure. This process occurs largely outside of our conscious awareness.

This means that most of us without even realizing it have taken some of our very human and natural impulses, feelings and desires and cast them into the darkness—or shadows of our existence. Whether we have stuffed difficult emotions (e.g., anger, sadness or selfishness) or seemingly positive ones (e.g., playfulness, intuition and sensuality), we have pushed energetic experiences below our conscious awareness where they are left to assert their influence in hidden ways.

Shadows can be slippery and sneaky, and they generally find their way towards expression. Often they emerge through our own destructive behaviors and our interactions with the people in our lives. In fact, the very people that trigger us the most are often the ones who are acting out the same impulses and desires we've suppressed.

THE SACRED ROLE OF THE SHADOW

The shadow is like the nugget of coal that may hide a diamond of great beauty.

~ Richard Rudd

Shadows may be slippery and sneaky, but they are also sacred if we learn to embrace them. The attitude we hold towards our own suffering is ultimately what determines whether our *Shadows* serve us and humanity, or not.

Some questions for you to contemplate when experiencing a painful, uncomfortable or forbidden feeling:

Do you push the feeling away?
Do you judge it?
Do you feel victimized by it?
Do you blame others for it?

Or, can you allow it to be what it is?

Can you let yourself fully feel it—allowing it
to wash through you,
while keeping your heart open?

Can you stay, breathe and trust?

So here is my invitation to you... Every time you fall into a *Shadow* space, hold it as *holy ground*. Don't try to do anything to it. Just allow it to be. Become fully present to the perfection of whatever you are experiencing. A perfect pain. A perfect confusion. A perfect agony. The more you can do just that, the more you will find yourself—naturally—expanding into the realm of the *Gift*.

When you are feeling most alone and burdened by your personal pain, realize that you are profoundly connected to the pain of the world. Just like the *Wisdom Keepers*, you are designed to hold a piece of the grand human tapestry of experience. When you understand, metabolize and transform a particular aspect of human suffering, you do so for the sake of the world. When you heal your own pain, you help to heal the pain of humanity.

The Wisdom Keepers Oracle Deck makes a wonderful learning supplement for *Gene Keys* (and *Human Design*) enthusiasts. Given that the *Gene Keys* represent a vast body of knowledge and are intellectually rigorous, this deck offers people an additional way to glean the essence—one that is direct, intimate, relational and heart-opening.

In each *Wisdom Keeper* story, you will find that *Gene Keys*-related keywords are italicized.

The cards have also been color-coded for those who want to work intentionally with Richard Rudd's *21 Codon Rings* from *The Gene Keys*, or *Wisdom Keeper* 'soul groups.'

(See the Final Note at the end of this guidebook for more information about the Color Code.)

How to Approach the Wisdom Keepers

Using a deck like this can add a dimension of playfulness and synchronicity to your explorations. As you explore the faces in *The Wisdom Keepers Oracle Deck*, remain open and receptive. You may find yourself feeling particularly drawn to one *Wisdom Keeper*... or more. Trust there is a reason for this. There is transformative power in your connection. Remember, it is impossible to make a mistake or receive the wrong *Wisdom Keeper*.

When working with the cards, I encourage you to place your *Wisdom Keepers* in a special place that you frequently visit. Every time you connect with these beings, know that you are connecting with yourself, an archetypal essence, and your life's profound potential. There is magic in the eyes.

Whenever shuffling or pulling a card, hold a question and intention in your heart. Ask for the right *Wisdom Keepers* to come to you, and that your *Wisdom Keeper*, or card spread, serve your highest good. Consider using your non-dominant hand to pull the cards— to evoke the wisdom of your inner child, and help you release the mind.

Keep your questions open-ended, as opposed to yes/no questions. Keep them practical and grounded in the Now. (This Oracle Deck is not intended to be used as a predictive device.)

You are invited to keep a *Wisdom Keeper* journal where you can gather reflections, insights, images and unfolding dreams as you go. When you choose a *Wisdom Keeper*, you might want to go directly to the Guidebook to learn about that *Wisdom Keeper* and be inspired by the questions and action steps provided. Or, you might want to spend time with the *Wisdom Keeper* on your own before consulting the Guidebook, to see what intuitive guidance you receive without outer influence. Trust yourself to know what you need.

Use these additional questions to support your contemplations:

What does this particular
Wisdom Keeper inspire in you?

What important truth does he or she
remind you of?

Which of your *Gifts* does this *Wisdom Keeper*
see and trust?

Which of your *Shadows* might this being
understand and embrace?

If this *Wisdom Keeper* had a message for you today,
what would it be?

If you were to sit down and have a conversation
with this person, what would you want to share?
What would you want to ask?
How do you imagine she or he would respond?

And remember...

Listen...Relax...in every way.
Physically, emotionally and mentally.
Soften and melt your heart. Let go of the need to understand this logically
in the Now, and give your mind permission to learn over time.

With each Wisdom Keeper you will find:

A Number: Each *Wisdom Keeper* is associated with one of 64 archetypes, which can be related to the 64 hexagrams of the I Ching and some of its descendants, including the 64 *Gene Keys*.

Three Words (*Gift, Shadow* and *Siddhi, as described earlier*) **and a Programming Partner**: Just as each *Gene Key* has a *Programming Partner*, each *Wisdom Keeper* has a companion or soul friend. Together they reflect a paradox as well as a totality. I encourage you to intuitively explore the partnerships, and allow them to inspire you. Richard Rudd expands on *Gift, Shadow, Siddhi* and *Programming Partner* in his book, *The Gene Keys*.

Symbols: Each face has been intentionally infused with universal yet specific symbols, reflecting the unique *Gifts* embodied by the *Wisdom Keeper*.

A Wisdom Story: Each *Wisdom Keeper* shares an archetypal yet deeply personal story. You will notice that none of the *Wisdom Keepers* have arrived at the place they are today without experiencing their own form of suffering and without embracing a *Shadow*.

A Gift for You: Each *Wisdom Keeper* brings you a gift of wisdom and guidance. The *Gift* is offered through words that come straight from the heart.

Questions for Contemplation: Contemplation is one of the most gentle yet powerful ways to catalyze a deep transformation in your life. Simple yet poignant questions are offered to help you connect with the *Wisdom Keepers* and their stories, and to integrate their guidance into your own life through practical action steps.

The

Wisdom Keepers

Speak...

1

FRESHNESS

The genius of freshness is to bring something to the world that no other has ever seen before.

Gift: Freshness
Shadow: Entropy
Siddhi: Beauty
Programming Partner: 2

~Richard Rudd

MY WISDOM STORY

People say I was born with a big smile on my face. But as I grew up, I'd suddenly feel sad and *depressed*, without warning, and it scared me. I wanted that low feeling to go away. So I tried to get rid of it. I avoided it, judged it, tried to 'cathart' it, then to fix it. I even tried to predict it, and got pretty good at explaining it. But I still couldn't control it. The gloom came whenever it felt like coming, never asking for my permission.

For a while I managed to push the pain away by keeping myself nice and busy. I *frenetically* filled my calendar and life with people and activities. But eventually I burned out from all of that busyness. There were days, weeks, even months I couldn't get out of bed. I felt numb, like my life was deteriorating and taken over by *entropy*. I was convinced something was terribly wrong with my feelings, and with me for having them, and I was certain that my sadness was keeping me from creating the life I knew I should have.

One day, out of pure desperation, I gave up on judging and fighting the melancholy. And the strangest thing happened. It just went away, in its own sweet time, like a cloud floating by—as if it were the most natural thing in the world. And then, to my delight, my creativity peeked out like the sun.

Now I allow myself plenty of alone time, to simply be. I see my low moments as natural parts of life. I embrace them fully, without overanalyzing. The less hard I work at it, the more I find joy and aliveness rising up from within me, as well as a natural desire to express that joy in a creative way. I now trust that it is actually healthy for me to burst forth with *Freshness* and enthusiasm when joy appears, and then to withdraw and enjoy my solitude when my creative rumblings pull me inward. I have the best impact that way.

My Gift to You

When I look at you and you're feeling down, I know that nothing is innately wrong. Your wise body is recharging, and something deep and creative is growing in your beautiful belly. Please do not worry if you don't have a clue about what's being born. Just do your best to trust and allow for your feelings, and take a little 'me time.' Soon enough, you will feel renewed and ready to burst out into the world with *Freshness* and a new perspective. The more you learn how to embrace your sadness with open arms, the more energized people will feel when they are around you. They will see the light and fire in your soul. Remember, the aliveness and *Beauty* you see in me are in you, too. Your Joy is more resilient and contagious than you can even imagine. And its timing is perfect. So embrace where you are, and trust that your bright light will always appear just when it can have its most inspiring impact.

QUESTIONS FOR CONTEMPLATION

- Do you often find yourself judging, overanalyzing or trying to get rid of certain feelings? How does this impact your body?
- Which of your feelings do you tend to push away the most because of its heaviness?
- Find a way to give yourself total permission to have and express this feeling today. Write about it in your journal; share about it with someone you trust; listen to a song or watch a movie that captures it; make a simple feeling collage. Whatever you do, give it space and see what happens.
- What simple act would bring more *Beauty* into your life today?

ORIENTATION

As you come more into contact with your unity with all creatures, you also witness an enhancement in your own uniqueness, particularly through your creative process.

Gift: Orientation
Shadow: Dislocation
Siddhi: Unity
Programming Partner: 1

~Richard Rudd

MY WISDOM STORY

As a child, the trees were my friends and the animals were my family. To my people, everything was connected and pulsing with life. But then my family moved to a world of straight lines and tiny boxes. I felt different, cut off, and *dislocated*. Every turn I took seemed wrong.

So I discarded my indigenous roots and started collecting human friends, money and knowledge. I even dabbled in Western religions, until I chose modern science as my God. My life became structured, ordered and *regimented*. On the surface, I laughed at my parents' chaotic, irrational ways. But underneath, I felt helpless, out of sync and full of self-doubt. At night, I had recurring nightmares of humanity self-destructing.

At one point, I felt so *lost* I considered ending my life. But then my grandmother passed away. The following night, she came to me in a dream and said, "Every time you reject your roots, my sweet boy, you not only reject me and our family, but the entire cosmos." That dream did something to me. Something powerful. The very next day I found myself planning a trip back to Australia. It would be the first time I visited since our family moved away.

The moment I got off the plane, a flood of old feelings rushed through me. It was as if the land entered my bloodstream, and my body remembered how it felt to trust, surrender and let go. Ironically, it was also in that moment that I realized that there was nothing I needed to do, nowhere I needed to go in order to end the sense of lostness and emptiness that had ruled my life. Simply becoming aware of the longings underneath was enough to reorient and renew me with a surge of unexpected creativity.

Now I know in my whole body that I belong, no matter where I am, and that I have something wonderfully unique to contribute. Even in the busy city, the trees are my friends and everything around me is part of a beautiful symphony, where I am playing a unique and essential instrument.

MY GIFT TO YOU

I come to bring you the Gift of *Orientation*. When you look into my eyes, allow me to remind you of the deepest truth—that we are all ONE. You and I may look different from each other, but deep down, we are the same. Care less about what others think of you, and more about how you are a natural part of the whole. Open yourself up to a path of synchronicity as you surrender into my eyes. Don't think too much. Allow the certainty within me—that we are all connected in a single *Unity*, that all things happen in the exact right timing—to reassure you that there is no way for you to be outside of the stream of Life. It is simply not possible.

Questions for Contemplation

- Are you feeling *lost*, alone or out of sync?
- Or are you constantly trying to control, define or *regiment* your life?
- When did you last feel a deep sense of *Unity*—like you were in the flow and connected to all of life? Where were you? Who were you with?
- Find a simple way to reconnect with that feeling today. Spend time in nature. Sing, dance or laugh with others. Go to a favorite place, and take it all in.

INNOVATION

*Who, what and wherever you are, if you are not
continually transcending, then you are dying.*

Gift: Innovation
Shadow: Chaos
Siddhi: Innocence
Programming Partner: 50

~ Richard Rudd

My Wisdom Story

Like all children, I love to play. Sometimes what I'm doing seems—to the adults around me—to be creating nothing more than a bunch of *chaos* and *disorder*. It makes them nervous, because I rarely know what's going to happen when I'm playing, or where it's going to lead. But I don't care about that. Because all I want to do is express myself and have an adventure.

I actually love the feeling of changing my environment, and then being changed by it in return. And because I always keep my heart as open as my mind, I prefer to play with people who love a mystery as much as I do, who are up for getting into trouble, so that we can find our way out of it.

Sometimes when I'm playing with my friends or my imagination, something scary shows up, like a monster. At first, we never know what we're going to do. But then, we put our heads and hearts together and come up with some fantastic plan to save ourselves and the whole world, which usually involves putting all sorts of things and people and beings together that no one would ever think of. Or, we shriek, throw our hands up in the air, and end up dancing with the monster. Either way, our fears usually turn into some kind of fun.

We rarely bother with questions like, "Is that monster real or not?" Or, "Will a combination of laser beams and cotton candy really work as a monster destabilizer?" When we're playing, we're not worrying about any of that. No television, parent or teacher could ever convince us about what's true, or possible, or reasonable or practical, or what isn't. Or what goes together, and what doesn't. All that matters is that we save the world, do something awesome together, and enjoy ourselves along the way.

MY GIFT TO YOU

Don't be fooled. I am young, but wise. I come when it's time to embrace all new beginnings with a full, adventure-loving and innocent heart. And to discover how much more powerful and transformative your contribution to this world of ours can be. I am an agent of change, synthesis and *Innovation*. When I look into your eyes, I see where you're still not trusting life. Let me tell you a secret. We are all built for change. Just like the flowers infused in my face, you, too, are meant to constantly bloom and wilt, and bloom again. So there is no need to control and avoid *chaos* at every turn. For that would be like trying to protect yourself against the Cosmos itself, or your own ever-evolving nature. Whatever ideas, dogmas or beliefs you have, let them go. At least for this moment. Instead, have some fun. Improvise. Say YES to whatever is happening, add an unexpected spice to the collaborative soup, and enjoy the magnificent ride, no matter where it leads you.

Questions for Contemplation

- Does your life often feel *disordered* and *chaotic*, or do you tend towards being '*anal*,' always trying to maintain control?
- When faced with *chaos*, how do you (and your body) respond?
- Are you afraid of an inner or outer change?
- What would you do differently if you made friends with the unknown, instead of resisting it?
- Connect with a time in your life when you felt *innocent* and childlike.
- What new adventure awaits you?
- What area of your life is calling out for *Innovation*?

UNDERSTANDING

True understanding lies outside the domain of the mind.

Gift: Understanding
Shadow: Intolerance
Siddhi: Forgiveness
Programming Partner: 49

~ Richard Rudd

My Wisdom Story

I was born into this world with the blessing and curse of a sharp mind. You might not know this looking at me now, but when I was young, I was always working so hard to understand everything. Always digging up reasons for why I felt the way I felt, and why I should trust and act on my emotions, no matter how fearful, angry or prejudiced they were. My mind was constantly chewing, explaining, justifying and *nit-picking*. I became increasingly intolerant of people whose *understanding* seemed simple, or whose world views were different than my own.

Sometimes the arguments and counter-arguments in my mind became so exhausting that the energy drained completely out of my body. During those times, beneath my seeming *apathy*, lived a profound insecurity. The truth was that I felt horribly anxious when I couldn't find logical answers to my questions.

But that was at a time when thinking ruled my life. That was when I still believed that my mind was capable of fulfilling my desires, relieving my fears, and bringing me the peace and security I yearned for.

It wasn't until I fully embraced life's uncertainty that I stopped needing to defend my viewpoint. That's when I discovered that true *Understanding* had nothing to do with intellectual knowledge, but instead was meant to infuse the whole body and open the heart.

Now I no longer get stuck on one side of an issue or spend precious energy defending my point of view. I enjoy seeing every situation from all sides. I joyfully use the brilliance of my mind to help others reach beyond the limitations of their biases and *intolerances*, and help them see a bigger picture. In the end, the true purpose of the mind is to bring *Forgiveness* to the heart.

MY GIFT TO YOU

When I look at you, and I watch you struggling to figure out your life, form your opinions, or defend your feelings, I hold you with love and patience. I am here to invite you to use your beautiful mind to do what it's best at. Let it play, research, communicate and serve this world of ours. Let it build bridges of compassion, and help people learn how to release their biases and intolerances, so that we can all see and celebrate the bigger picture. I know and trust that at some point, your hard-working mind will exhaust itself, and you will break free into a new way of being, where true *Understanding* fills your belly and emanates from your heart. For now, I ask that you begin by forgiving yourself. Soon you will no longer doubt that you—and the whole wide world—are so much more worthy and wonderful than what your busy mind could ever comprehend.

Questions for Contemplation

- Do you tend to over-think and *nit-pick*, or become paralyzed with indecision?

- Are there certain things, situations and people you feel you just have to understand, or you can't relax?

- In what situations do you find yourself *intolerant* of others? Can you forgive yourself (and others) for closing your heart?

- Think of a time when you experienced true *Understanding*. Or *Forgiveness*.

- How can you tell when you are thinking with your heart? Reflect upon these questions in your journal.

PATIENCE

Patience is about Trust... If you trust in life, you will trust life in every moment, even the challenging moments, and in so doing you will always remain in the flow.

Gift: Patience
Shadow: Impatience
Siddhi: Timelessness
Programming Partner: 35

~ Richard Rudd

MY WISDOM STORY

When I was a young man, I was always in a hurry. My breath was shallow and my nerves on edge. No matter how things seemed on the outside, I always felt that something was wrong on the inside. I owned a small grocery store, but had my sights on something bigger. I believed that if I didn't make things happen, they wouldn't. My destiny was all up to me. Time was running out, and I was failing.

There were times when I was so *impatient* and desperate for my business to grow that I became very *pushy*. So *pushy* that my staff quit, suppliers refused to work with me, and customers stopped coming. In my despair, I became consumed with *pessimism*, believing nothing would ever work out for me, no matter how hard I tried. But then one evening, when I was sitting alone and wondering whether I should give it all up, a kind old man knocked on the gate. He held the Book of Changes in one hand, and a tiny tree in the other—so beautiful it glowed. I let him in, and the two of us sat down together and talked for hours. I lost track of all time. Next thing I knew, I was agreeing to become his apprentice and learn the sacred arts of I Ching divination and Penjing (Chinese Bonsai).

That was many years ago. Now I can laugh as I acknowledge just how much *patience* it took me to learn *Patience*. How many times my master had to remind me to slow down, breathe deeply, and accept whatever was happening in my life. There was no need to manipulate, conquer or collapse. He taught me to treasure nature, flow with the seasons, and that a similar, perfect and orderly rhythm lived and moved in my own soul. Yin would always turn to yang, and yang would always return to yin. *Patience* paid off. My teacher and the trees taught me to trust in life, to honor each moment, even the hardest, most painful ones. Now my life is simple, and I often enjoy the most delicious states of *Timelessness*.

My Gift to You

It is time to soften your shoulders and relax your breath. Get quiet. Listen to your own heartbeat. There is nothing you have to do right now. Life is deeply intelligent. Its timing is impeccable; it always knows what's best for you. And you, my friend, are an intricate part of Life, forever-connected to everyone and everything around you. I am here to remind you that nothing happens by accident or without a potential gift. A delayed train can lead to an unexpected encounter. A personal crisis can birth a healing opportunity. An individual's pain can unleash collective transformation. And all with perfect timing. So take another deep breath, step out of the way, and befriend *Patience*. Your Soul will thank you for it.

Questions for Contemplation

- Where in your life—and with whom—are you feeling most *impatient?*

- If you fully trusted in Life's perfect timing, and that nothing happens accidentally, how might your thoughts, feelings, attitudes and relationships change? What might you do—or not do—differently?

- Remember the last time you experienced a sense of *Timelessness.* Where were you?

- See if you can BE more and hurry (and worry!) less today. If you experience an uncomfortable feeling, tell yourself, "I'm embracing this feeling for all of humanity."

DIPLOMACY

Emotional maturity means that your awareness operates even during the most profound emotional states.

Gift: Diplomacy
Shadow: Conflict
Siddhi: Peace
Programming Partner: 36

~ Richard Rudd

My Wisdom Story

Where I grew up, tragedy and violence were all that we knew. Generations of my people had been traumatized and scarred, and *conflict* was everywhere—between West and East, modern and ancient, wealthy and poor, men and women.

As a young girl, I had little power. I could neither speak out against the injustices I witnessed in the world nor the abuses that happened at home. Always afraid of attack, my body was on a constant state of alert. On the outside, I was *over-attentive*. The *peacemaker*. At any sign of *conflict*, I'd smooth out the waters. But on the inside, I was nervous and insecure. I feared all men, and people that were different from my own. I put up walls around my heart.

Once, I lost control and lashed out, blaming my father for being a bully, and my mother for being a victim, blaming entire nations for harming my people, and my people for letting them. My *tactless* words cut like knives. Overcome with guilt and fear, I begged for forgiveness, spending the next weeks punishing myself, and pleasing everyone around me. But the incessant pleasing—like the ruthless blaming—only made things worse.

It wasn't until I was invited to visit a local *Peace* group by my Great Aunt that everything changed. I'd never seen men and women sitting together, listening, supporting and inspiring each other with such open hearts, honesty and respect. They were neither guarded nor reactive. And for the first time, I experienced the kind of *peace* and love I'd been longing for my whole life. In the safety of my aunt's embrace, my defenses dropped. I finally faced the pain, powerlessness and loneliness I'd been hiding from myself and everyone else. I became the leader of this organization for many years. But now I find that *Peace* simply happens wherever I go.

My Gift to You

I am here to invite you to drop your defenses. Let down your guard. Stop fighting against your own humanity by refusing to see, feel and accept your inner demons. There is a way to calm emotional waters in your intimate relationships, and in the world, without repressing or avoiding the truth. There is a way to dissolve seemingly insurmountable barriers to *Peace*, to know precisely when it's time to act, when it's time to speak, and how to speak powerfully yet from the heart. The true path of *Peace* and *Diplomacy* requires that you fearlessly look at and embrace your own weaknesses. Don't protect yourself from your deepest emotions, and you will find that your timing, communication and relationships will improve. Naturally, others will want to confide in you, and you will sense just what is needed. Even in the most emotionally volatile situations. Your very presence can have the power to shift the energy of a room or a relationship, from one of *conflict* to *Peace*.

QUESTIONS FOR CONTEMPLATION

• Do you tend to avoid uncomfortable feelings through *peacemaking*, or by overreacting and exacerbating *conflict*?

• Is there a current *conflict* in your life, or a place where you are feeling defensive and your guard is up?

• What do you fear might happen if you stopped working so hard to please certain people?

• How can you take more responsibility for your feelings, and express them in less reactive and more open, honest ways?

• In what area of your life is a little *Diplomacy* needed?

• What is a simple way you can cultivate *Peace* in your life today?

GUIDANCE

The real leader is the ultimate listener.

Gift: Guidance
Shadow: Division
Siddhi: Virtue
Programming Partner: 13

~ Richard Rudd

My Wisdom Story

When I was little, I trusted and admired the peace-loving elders in my community. As I grew, my people experienced more oppression from the outside world, and new leaders appeared who believed that it was time to fight fire with fire.

At first, I *hid*. I handed my authority over to the elders who maintained the peaceful ways of our ancestors. But when our community was attacked, again and again, I handed my authority over to the leaders who fought back. I watched them become more and more like our enemies as *divisiveness* grew in our village. I was tired of giving my power away to *dictator* types, who never bothered to ask what I thought or how I felt. I was tired of waiting for others to get it right. So I stepped forward as a leader and fought for my people and for justice everywhere.

Over the years, I attracted many followers. Always certain I was on the right side of justice, a deep ambition grew in me that was fueled by an anger I hadn't yet owned. One day I scolded a young woman for not listening to me or following my advice. Her tears showed me I had lost my way. From that day on, I stopped leading and started listening. I discovered that every community member was wise and capable of making an important contribution to our people's path.

Today I am no longer fueled by a fear of oppression, or the desire for external recognition. I don't need everyone to understand the way I lead, or why I do what I do. What drives me now is a deep love of service, and the belief that there is no such thing as a healthy community without healthy, free and autonomous individuals.

When I guide groups, I interfere as little as possible, and always find that each person's wisdom and gifts just naturally rise to the surface. The less I push my agenda for the group, the deeper the communication, the more transformative the action, and the smoother the implementation of the vision becomes. There will be more and more leaders like me as we move into the future. I know this to be true. Thus I am able to trust in humanity, even during these turbulent times.

MY GIFT TO YOU

I am here to share that true leadership is not about forcefully imposing an agenda or interfering in others' lives. It is about lovingly empowering from behind the scenes. Be not driven by the fear of oppression or the love of power, but by a profound love of service. I am here to provide you with true *Guidance*. I come to recognize the wise, free leader in you, and to help you trust in your own direction. I am listening.

Questions for Contemplation

- Where—to whom—are you giving your power away? Where are you still *hiding*?
- Who has given you their power? Is it time to give it back?
- Are there areas in your life where you're pushing your agenda? Are you willing to listen more deeply to the needs of others?
- How is it that you would most love to serve this world?
- Where is your loving *Guidance* most needed now?
- Think of someone in your life who has acted as an empowering, compassionate and *virtuous guide*. What were the qualities you loved most about this person? Pick one to intentionally integrate into your way of being, listening and doing today.

STYLE

Style is more than skin deep.
It is the cutting edge of creation itself.

Gift: Style
Shadow: Mediocrity
Siddhi: Exquisiteness
Programming Partner: 14

~ Richard Rudd

MY WISDOM STORY

When I was a little girl, I sang everywhere I went and all of the time. I was so full of music it just burst out of me. My mother raised me on her own. She was deaf, so couldn't hear me sing, although she could see the surprised and offended looks on people's faces when we went out together. She herself had worked so hard to fit in that she felt embarrassed by my singing, and worried for me. So she shushed me when we went out, and put me in a school where singing was forbidden. I instinctively understood she was trying to protect me. And I loved her. So I learned to swallow my voice and blend in.

I became just like everyone else—a pleasant student, an unthreatening classmate, an obedient daughter and a model of *mediocrity*. I followed all of the rules. My teachers liked me. My mother was proud. And as a young woman, I had everything I was taught to want. A respectable and substantial place in the world. Manicured nails. The latest fashions. A respectable job.

But it was all *artificial*. When yet another marriage fell apart, I couldn't deny the truth anymore. I wasn't happy. I felt trapped, almost *wooden*. On the surface my life seemed shiny, but it was flat. Nothing truly glowed. Until I found myself walking past a park that was filled with all kinds of people, the kind I normally avoided like the plague. They were drumming and dancing in a circle with such abandon that they didn't seem to care if anybody was watching. Someone grabbed me by the hand, and I found myself leaping into the center of the circle, and the next thing I knew my eyes closed, body swayed and my own voice started ringing out. I felt alive again. I was too happy and terrified to hear the applause.

That was long ago. It took me many years to integrate the courage I experienced that day, to work through my fears of both succeeding and failing. Now, of course, I sing everywhere and all the time—whenever my rebel soul moves me to. And I think just as freely as I sing.

MY GIFT TO YOU

I have a hunch there is a voice in you longing to be heard. I am here to encourage you to stop worrying about blending in. Dare to be an original. Don't just follow the trends. Be a rebel with a cause. Embrace your own *Style*, and let it come from deep inside. When I see you doing something that others may think is crazy or 'too much,' I know that you are as sane as sane could be. Maybe there are people who won't stick around. I understand how painful that can be. I also promise you, there will be others who will be so inspired by your *Style* that they'll catch the authenticity bug. So please, get comfortable with being a fringe dweller. Trust that the world will catch up with you, in its own good time. No matter what your passion is, give it some air. Set it free. And expect nothing less than *Exquisiteness*.

QUESTIONS FOR CONTEMPLATION

- In what ways did you learn to blend in, to be like everyone else?
- Where are you still blending in, but secretly wanting to leap out?
- What would you do if you weren't afraid of what others would think of you? Is there a risk you've been longing to take, in service of a passion, but you've been afraid of failure (or success)? What is your fear?
- Where can you receive support and encouragement?
- How can you coax out your individual, creative *Style*?
- Complete the sentence: "When I am in my *Exquisiteness*, I am..." Repeat as many times as you like, and write what emerges in your journal.

DETERMINATION

All those little acts done with heart begin to build up an inner momentum that eventually becomes unstoppable.

Gift: Determination
Shadow: Inertia
Siddhi: Invincibility
Programming Partner: 16

~ Richard Rudd

My Wisdom Story

I always knew I was meant to be a Goddess, and couldn't wait to find that passionate calling and perfect romance. I dismissed the unglamorous steps I was told were necessary to achieve my goals. I thought them boring. In a frenzy to get through the Now so I could get to the future, I hurled myself in one exciting direction (and relationship) after another, each time expecting my dreams to immediately manifest. But when they didn't, I'd quickly *divert* myself with a new enchanting vision.

For years, I was restless and antsy. I left all relationships the moment the honeymoon was over. I found myself wasting more and more of my time with meaningless activities, until I became so demoralized that I decided to give up my dreams entirely and settle for a 'normal life.' Instead of traveling the world with a jet-setting wizard, I married a dear friend and became a stay-at-home mom. Though I loved my family, my life became unbearably mundane. I wasn't just judging the small inconsequential moments; I was lost in *inertia*. Swallowed by endless tasks and responsibilities, my life felt devoid of hope and passion.

As my children grew older, and I experienced more pockets of spaciousness, hints of old dreams would pop up. But I'd quickly push them away, convincing myself I couldn't do 'Mommy' and 'Goddess' at the same time. Besides, I was too unfocused and *reluctant* to leave my comfort zone. But then, for Mother's Day, my family painted a picture of me dressed in full Goddess regalia, holding a broom, a paint brush and surrounded by laughing children. They called the art piece, Goddess Camp. As I looked into their loving faces, a lightbulb went on, and I knew what I was meant to do. Of course, it took time, effort and an abundance of small (and unglamorous) steps to get the camp up and running. But now I experience each step as an essential part of a grand adventure. And I couldn't be more fulfilled.

MY GIFT TO YOU

It's time to bring your heart back into everything you do, no matter how seemingly mundane. Remember, every act of intention is an act of magic. True *Determination* isn't about force or struggle. It's about grounding yourself in your heart's desire. It's about building natural momentum, one love-filled act at a time. Perhaps at the beginning of an endeavor, when you're dealing with inner *reluctance* or habitual diversions, you may need to assert some will. But once you start moving, the entire Universe (including your body) will rise up to meet you, creating a current of support to which you only need to surrender. Soon you will see the connection between every moment of your life and your deepest dreams. So listen to your heart. Prioritize the Practical, or the Beautiful. And let go of the rest. It's that simple.

QUESTIONS FOR CONTEMPLATION

- Do you tend to feel lost in the mundane, or are you often trying to escape it?
- Where do you desire more movement in your life? Who might help you burst through the *inertia* and get moving?
- If you've lost touch with a dream, find three ways to spend time with Beauty today. Move your body.
- If you've been frantically avoiding the practical, choose three simple tasks to complete, and find the magic in them. Then have a good rest.
- When do you remember feeling *Invincible*? Write down (or doodle) what it felt like in your journal.

NATURALNESS

Once you understand that you are neither your name or your actions, feelings, thoughts or beliefs, you realize that human nature is something far greater and wider than you ever suspected.

Gift: Naturalness
Shadow: Self-obsession
Siddhi: Being
Programming Partner: 15

~ Richard Rudd

My Wisdom Story

My parents and my culture always prioritized the collective over the individual. As a young girl, I mastered the arts of *self-denial* and invisibility. I lived through—and for—the people around me.

Over time, I started to feel like I was drowning, like I couldn't breathe, until an anger rumbled so loudly within me I could no longer deny it. Suddenly, my survival no longer depended on my disappearing. It depended on my ability to reject my family and conditioning at all costs. I could no longer risk losing myself, so I became obsessed with myself. I wanted to know myself, be myself, dress like myself, act like myself, even pray and commune with Spirit like myself. I looked to the West to show me how to be a true individual.

I became so good at being *Me* that no one could penetrate my fortress of selfhood, or my heart. I couldn't afford to be sensitive, or to care how my way of being impacted others. I believed most people wanted to change or trap me. The rest of them needed changing themselves.

It wasn't until all of my relationships fell apart that I realized just how *narcissistic* I'd become. It took courage to see and own just how angry, paranoid and impenetrable I was, and how, in my fear of losing myself, I'd been pushing people away.

Today I feel great compassion for myself and all beings who suffer as we struggle to find our way in life, to live out our true nature. It took me years to feel safe enough to let go of all of the identity trappings I gathered along the way, and to fully grasp that my true nature is beyond all definition.

Now I know that we can only experience and operate as a Unity if we allow ourselves to be our unique, *natural* selves.

MY GIFT TO YOU

I see you striving to discover who you are, and I know how difficult it can be to answer this deeply human question. While you're searching for your self, do not forget to enjoy the journey. There will be a time when you can just let it all go. In the end, you are not what you do or what you know. You are not your thoughts, feelings or beliefs. Nor are you your looks or job description. Over time, as this truth sinks in, and as you stop arguing with your life, you will find yourself becoming more grounded, centered and full of joy. More relaxed, free and at ease. Whatever is in your heart, whatever you're meant to do or express, will simply arise out of you with *Naturalness*. I am here to remind you that you are far more splendid than your mind could ever grasp, and your authentic nature is destined to bloom and contribute to the magnificent garden of which we're all a part. Graciously take a bow, get out of your own way, and let it happen.

QUESTIONS FOR CONTEMPLATION

- Where are you compromising or losing yourself in others?
- Where are you *self-obsessed*, or clinging too tightly to an identity, a way of thinking, being or doing?
- Where might you still be playing the martyr? Where do you need to stop compromising?
- Think of a time you experienced true *Naturalness*, when you fully relaxed in your own skin? What about that situation brought out the *Naturalness* in you?
- In what ways can you expand your sense of self, of *Being*? Write your reflections in your journal.

IDEALISM

The only thing needed for magic to occur is some form of structure and an open mind.

Gift: Idealism
Shadow: Obscurity
Siddhi: Light
Programming Partner: 12

~ Richard Rudd

My Wisdom Story

At home, I was always encouraged to indulge in my imagination. I was constantly dreaming up and acting out stories. And it was wonderful. At school, however, when I got caught staring out the window, I was told to take my head out of the clouds, pay attention and be realistic. So I quickly learned to keep my fantasies to myself.

For a long time, no one knew how little I cared about 'real' life, which in comparison to my *fantasy* life, seemed completely devoid of wonder. But my parents sensed something was off. They began to worry. They took me to an even more concerned doctor, who prescribed some pills and behavioral techniques to end the delusions and bring me back to the world.

For a while it seemed to work, and I was able to get off the medicine. But slowly my imagination kicked back in. This time, instead of keeping my dreams to myself, I desperately tried to manifest them. But they could never measure up to my original ideals. Powerless and angry, I tried to push them away again. But this time, the more I tried to bury my *fantasies*, the darker and more *obscure* they got. The demons from my dreams became the people I dated. I kept recreating the same awful situations, especially in my intimate relationships. It got so bad I wanted to escape life entirely.

Luckily, I had a dream one night where a polar bear walked right up to me with a golden journal, pen and paints in his mouth. The next day I ran to the store and started the first of what would be hundreds of art journals. I drew pictures, wrote poems and painted all of the feelings and visions I'd been afraid to own. I learned to trust in the images that came to me. Now I always provide a free-range outlet for my imagination. And I find that just naturally, I am embodying and manifesting my deepest dreams.

MY GIFT TO YOU

I am here to remind you of the incredible power and potential of your receptive, abundant, feminine, magical, tribal, dreaming mind. I come to give you permission to play with your right brain, with the realms of imagery, archetype and imagination. Trust that everything, in the end, is a symbol. Whatever comes to you, please do not judge it, over-identify with it, or squeeze it into a preconceived shape. And please don't judge yourself in any way for the unusual or optimistic contents of your imagination. In our modern world, many of us are taught to think of idealists as naïve, weak and *deluded* people—out of touch with reality. It is true that to manifest itself in the world, *Idealism* needs a structure. But without knowing our ideals or recognizing our dreams, how can we possibly manifest anything of true value? To bring our world back into balance, we need people like you to practice *magical realism*, where your beautiful open mind is honored just as much as the logical plans your brilliant left-brain might drum up!

QUESTIONS FOR CONTEMPLATION

- Do you tend to get too lost in *fantasy*, or not take your dreams seriously enough?
- Is it time to let go of a *fantasy* that's been keeping you from living and enjoying your actual life?
- Is it time to take an old (perhaps forbidden or 'unrealistic') dream out of the closet, and give it expression?
- Find a *Light* totem that holds an energy of one of your deepest dreams or ideals. Find a way to wear or carry it, so you can have it with you for as long as you want.

DISCRIMINATION

*To discriminate is to know inherently
what and who is healthy for you in life.*

Gift: Discrimination
Shadow: Vanity
Siddhi: Purity
Programming Partner: 11

~ Richard Rudd

My Wisdom Story

From birth, I was recognized as an old, wise soul. It pained me to see the brutality and maliciousness of humanity, and it was easy for me to see through the fears and folly of the people around me.

Instinctively I knew there was more to life, so I launched my spiritual search. For years, I studied with wise teachers, watched my thoughts and mastered my emotions. As I progressed, my mind became clear, my expressions artful, and my communication immaculate.

Everyone commented on my impressively calm and agreeable nature. I looked around me and saw people consumed by misguided efforts to look good and appear successful. I watched them blindly clinging to limited systems and beliefs, and I felt grateful that I was no longer caught up in such a sad, futile game.

Until it hit me. Beneath my gratitude was pride, and even deeper than that, a subtle and *elitist* disdain for those who hadn't achieved the level of spiritual awareness and non-attachment that I had.

The very *vanity* I saw in the world lived in me. With this realization came the next; the more I tried to transcend or reject my own *vanity*, the more subtly it shape-shifted and held fast to me. Once I befriended my very human need to feel special, I was able to appreciate its tremendous gifts, and the essential role it plays in our shared creative evolution.

MY GIFT TO YOU

I want you to know that *Vanity* is a necessary, beautiful part of being human. Without a love of your uniqueness, how could you possibly unfold your intelligent wings, rejoice in your personal power, or come to know and express your most wonderful qualities?

In the end, we will all discover that if we truly love ourselves, we must love everyone, for we are all One. But for now, I invite you to stop obsessing about what you can and should do to get rid of your *Vanity*. Instead, allow yourself to fall in love with your own authenticity, and the authenticity in others. Learn to *Discriminate* the real from the false, and who and what is healthy for you. Transform your innate desire to improve yourself into an art form. And speak from the heart. The rest will take care of itself.

QUESTIONS FOR CONTEMPLATION

• What masks do you wear in your every day life? What do you fear (or hope) might happen if you took off the mask?

- How does your inner *elitist* express itself? Do you sometimes think that you are more evolved than others? Do you keep these thoughts to yourself, or do they sometimes leak out with *malice*? Be honest.

- Do you have a good sense of *Discrimination*? Do you know who or what is healthy for you? How do you know this?

- Start listening to your voice when you speak. Notice how much of your *Pure* Heart is in what you say. If there's a lack of heart, there may be a form of *vanity* present that isn't serving you.

DISCERNMENT

Discernment begins at an individual level as you come to see how deeply your view of others is connected to your feelings. Over time, your personal agendas become more lucid and you reclaim the ability to listen to others and the world from a broader perspective.

Gift: Discernment
Shadow: Discord
Siddhi: Empathy
Programming Partner: 7

~ Richard Rudd

MY WISDOM STORY

I grew up in a fundamentalist household, to parents who were *narrow-minded*, opinionated and reactive. If I expressed something that didn't fit with their beliefs, or was too optimistic, they beat me down with words or a belt. They were always in the right, and I was always in the wrong. To survive their anger, bitterness and pessimism, I turned into water. I became soft, compliant and forever-yielding. I sacrificed my backbone in order to stay safe, and got so good at pretending to be sweet and kind that I forgot I was pretending.

As I entered womanhood, I became a *permissive* carpet, allowing others to walk all over me. And even though I had strong beliefs inside, I never stood up for what I believed in. I repeated this pattern, falling into one abusive relationship after another. All of my decisions were fueled by a desire for safety, even though I was rarely safe, and I was often surrounded by *discord*. I refused to do what I knew had to be done.

Until the day I saw my husband touching my daughter inappropriately. That was it. I could no longer deny my feelings, or refuse to act. The moment I was forced to listen to the rage, pain and utter hopelessness that had been living inside of me was the moment my true heroic life began. Now I watch the human drama playing out all around me, with *empathy*, compassion and optimism. I write myths and children's books that acknowledge the mythical journey that is the human life. All true heroes and heroines go through dark nights of the soul. Transformation and redemption are inevitable, when we are willing to wake up, *discern* and truly listen.

My Gift to You

I am here to wake you up. Where are you repeating the same mistakes? Where are you refusing to listen and accept the consequences of your heart's truth? You will be surprised at how courageous you are, once you begin to be honest with yourself. It is time to start listening—to yourself, and to others. Learn the art of *Discernment*. Listen beneath the words. Listen for the deeper desires, the emotional agenda, and the underlying tone. Listen beyond your own individual story. There is a grand mythic human drama playing out in your life, and all around you. We are all a part of it. We all have our version of the Underworld. We all carry the wand of a wizard, the sword of a warrior and the potential for a happy ending. As you begin to see the mythic quality of your own rich human life, your optimism will grow right along with your *Empathy*, compassion and heroic potential. You are not alone. I am here.

Questions for Contemplation

- Where are you trapped in a self-destructive cycle?
- Where are you starving for *Empathy*, from yourself, or others?
- *Discern* the ways that your experience of the world around you is colored by your mental and emotional states.
- How can you be more empathic towards yourself and others in your everyday life?
- Is there a myth you resonate with at a deep level? One that reflects your family or cultural story?
- If you were to write your own myth, what would it be about? Who would be the protagonist? Write a simple myth in your journal. Let the story impact your life.

COMPETENCE

Competence carries within it efficiency, enthusiasm, flair and flexibility—the four keys to material success.

Gift: Competence
Shadow: Compromise
Siddhi: Bounteousness
Programming Partner: 8

~ Richard Rudd

MY WISDOM STORY

I was born a prince, but my family was exiled from our country. To survive, my parents wiped the royalty out of our past. We became a normal family in a normal world. We lived in a modest home; I went to a conventional school; I was taught to want what everyone else wanted. And as I became a young man, I worked, like everyone else, to attain stability and success. I got married, studied hard and found respectable jobs. I made money and received recognition. Lots of recognition. I never loved what I did, nor did I expect to. What mattered was that I played by the rules, provided for my wife and was winning the game.

But as time passed and my status grew, so did a sinking feeling in my gut. I felt trapped and devoid of passion, as if something important was missing from my life. So my wife and I decided it was time to have children. But no matter how hard we tried, we couldn't conceive. The more frustrated, ashamed and *impotent* I felt, the harder I struggled to prove myself in the professional world. I was willing to *compromise* everything for success, including my health and the intimacy in my marriage.

As my wife and I drifted apart, my body began to suffer. Despite my stubborn attempts to deny my pain, my wife finally confronted me one night. Peering into my dulled eyes, she gripped my shoulders and exclaimed, "Enough! No more success! It's killing you. It's killing us. And it's never going to fill the hole inside of you." Then, with great tenderness and sincerity, she asked me what it was that I truly dreamed for myself, and for my life. If I wasn't worried about providing for her, or so *enslaved* by success, what did I truly want? In that moment, I realized I had never asked myself that question, in my entire life. Tears rolled down my face like an un-dammed river.

Together with my wife, I learned how to dream again. Eventually we grabbed hold of our souls, let go of the empire and embarked on an unexpected adventure. It was nothing less than pure enthusiasm that led us back home to my country of birth, and ultimately awakened my true *Competence*. Now I am far from normal—a King—devoted to serving and protecting thousands of returning child refugees. My wife and I love each other and all that we do. My enthusiasm is so contagious that the children can't help but follow their hearts.

MY GIFT TO YOU

I am here to remind you of your dreams, and to encourage you to take an honest look at your life. It is time to put the fire back into your belly, and to stop making *compromises*. The more you *compromise*, the more trapped you will become in a life that isn't even yours. You were born to inherit a rich, fulfilling and harmonious life, and to experience *Competence*. I see you cutting through obstacles, loving what you do, becoming a magnetic original, and adapting creatively to each new synchronistic opportunity that comes your way. Open to the *Bounteousness* that awaits!

QUESTIONS FOR CONTEMPLATION

- Where are you compromising in your life?
- Where are you settling?
- Where are you leaking precious energy?
- Think of a time you had fire in your belly.
- What does *Competence* mean to you? When have you felt the most competent in your life?
- Do you share the *Bounteousness* of your gifts with others?
- What dream is asking to be pulled out of the closet?
- Find a way to rekindle a dream and share your *Bounty* today.

MAGNETISM

One of the great challenges for modern humanity is to learn how to slow down.

Gift: Magnetism
Shadow: Dullness
Siddhi: Florescence
Programming Partner: 10

~ Richard Rudd

My Wisdom Story

We'd been living in that same small town forever. Maybe it was the muggy days or my hopping hormones, as Mom liked to say. But one summer, everything about that place rubbed me the wrong way. It wasn't that there was something horrible going on. It was that NOTHING was going on. I thought I'd die from the *dullness*. Either that, or strangle my sister for constantly trying to distract herself from the undeniable emptiness of our lives. My mom complained about my attitude. Maybe my sister couldn't stick with anyone or anything for more than five blinks at a time, and maybe her behavior was *extreme*, but at least she was trying. Me? I didn't care. I couldn't see the point of caring much about anything or anyone. My life was going nowhere.

But then I found myself looking at my dog Nilly. There she was, lounging on the porch, with her tongue hanging out, happy as a canine clam. At first I was green with envy. How on earth did she do that?! Just sit there, all relaxed, not needing to change a thing. And looking so annoyingly cute on top of it.

Next thing I knew I was lying down next to her, listening to the soft rise and fall of her furry belly, staring up at the sky, doing nothing… for hours. And in that timeless time, I bathed in so much *emptiness* that I started to overflow with a feeling that was better than happiness. Tears welled up and I squeezed Nilly until she could barely catch a pant. Since then, Mom says I'm giving off a glow. Even my sister is slowing down enough to hang out with me, even when there's nothing at all to do.

My Gift to You

If a country girl like me can find magic in the *dullest* places, so can you. But I'm here to tell you that you mustn't fight the *dullness*, or it won't work. You have to lean into it. You have to embrace it with your whole entire self. You have to slooooooow down. I know it's hard. It may even feel scary. But if you do that long enough, (without judging yourself for being lazy), you're very likely going to find yourself feeling pretty excited about life, and with an irresistible *Magnetism* gleaming out of your beautiful eyes. And you won't even need a reason for it.

Questions for Contemplation

• Do you try to escape *dullness* and feelings of *emptiness* through a flurry of activity that doesn't truly feed you?
• Or do you collapse into it through depression or resignation?
• What quality would you like to emanate from within?

- Do an experiment where you embrace *dullness* completely. Go for it. See what happens.

- Spend time with a completely relaxed animal. Learn from them.

- Think of someone you know who has deep personal *Magnetism*. How can their modeling help you to allow your own inner essence to shine?

VERSATILITY

The Gift of being versatile is the ability to pick up any skill that is needed and use it for a single aim—for the betterment of humanity and the service of the whole.

Gift: Versatility
Shadow: Indifference
Siddhi: Mastery
Programming Partner: 9

~ Richard Rudd

My Wisdom Story

I was hit by lightning as a boy. Our village shaman recognized this as a sign and took me under his wing. When the other children played, I learned about the healing property of plants, how to shake a rattle and beat a drum. Still, whenever possible, my heart drifted towards the sounds of laughing children and the stories told by the village grandmothers. At night I dreamed of cooking up food around crackling fires and telling stories that made young eyes go wide.

But when I awoke, I remembered who I was, and who I could never be. So I approached my shamanic training with obsessive discipline. I *deluded myself* into thinking I was on the right path, and that I wanted nothing else. There came a point where I had been initiated into all but the highest level of our ancient traditions.

It was time to receive the final initiation and accept my lifelong calling. But on the day of my ceremony, I panicked. I didn't feel ready, or good enough. I ran away into the woods. That night, surrounded by trees, I dreamt of the world falling apart, and myself powerless to save it. I returned to the village broken. I started neglecting my sacred duties and losing focus. I even started *gullibly* believing some of the messages leaking into our village from the surrounding cities, claiming that our small ancient ceremonies could never solve the problems of our wounded world.

My teacher saw the growing pessimism and *indifference* in my eyes. Finally, shaking, I confessed my soul's ache to serve the village, but in a different way. I couldn't accept my calling. To my surprise, he smiled and said, "You are indeed a shaman. Just a different kind. Listen to your dreams. Follow your heart. Take your new craft so deeply into your bones that you can use what you learn anywhere, with anyone, for any purpose." And so I did. Now whenever I appear, whatever I do, bellies hum, hearts lift and children laugh. I trust in my unique medicine. And I am happy.

MY GIFT TO YOU

When I look into your eyes, I see a great potential for talent and *Versatility*. I am here to remind you that, although talent requires persistent effort, everything gets easier when you take a stand for your true passion. Trust in your enthusiasm. Risk being different. Learn to let people down. I promise you, finding time to do what you love will get easier. Finding 'your people' will get easier. Asking for help will get easier. Sharing your fears will get easier. Even hard work will get easier, because everything you do will be fueled with love. Eventually your knowledge and skills will become such a deep part of you that you'll be playing and improvising with life itself. Service and Sustainability will just naturally happen. You are more ready than you know.

Questions for Contemplation

- Where have you given up on yourself and the world?
- What passions are you sitting on?
- Where are you telling yourself that you're not ready? What are you waiting for?
- What simple act could you take to turn a pipe dream into a reality-in-the-works?
- Have you convinced yourself there's no use, in relation to a particular passion of yours? What (and who) do you care enough about to find a way to serve anyway?
- Where do you have a natural talent? Think of one thing you can do to cultivate greater *Mastery* in that area.

FARSIGHTEDNESS

Far-sightedness can be said to arise directly out of the heart rather than from the mind.

Gift: Far-sightedness
Shadow: Opinion
Siddhi: Omniscience
Programming Partner: 18

~ Richard Rudd

MY WISDOM STORY

My parents needed me to accomplish great things, for the sake of our people. Even before school, I was quizzed and readied for intellectual excellence. Fact-gathering, test-taking and structured debating were praised, while irrational emotions were discouraged. My detail-prone eyes were trained to detect flaws. My critical, *opinionated* mind was honed on making comparisons, always pulling out the right fact to back up any theory.

My intellect served me well, as I became a good student, lawyer, then social critic. I did my research until I was certain about good, bad, right and wrong. My *opinions* were always on the side of justice and became increasingly humanitarian. To everyone I seemed unusually confident.

But deep down, I was serious, *self-critical* and took everything personally. I constantly compared myself to others, fearing they were more knowledgeable and accomplished. I had a deeply held *opinion* that without my achievements, I was unlovable. So I created an impenetrable shield and refused to use anything but logic to discuss anything, even in relational and emotional situations. Beneath my seemingly open-minded and progressive views, I was angry. I held onto my *opinions* like a fundamentalist. I lost friends over disagreements. But when I lost the love of my life over a stupid argument, I woke up. And from that moment on, my mind became the loyal, brilliant servant of my loving heart.

My Gift to You

I am here to remind you that nothing—no *opinion*, theory, dogma or belief—is more important than love. The only way to liberate yourself from the unhealthy grip of an *opinionated* life is to develop a sense of humor. True *Farsightedness* requires that you don't take yourself too seriously, or what anyone says too personally. Laugh more. It's not about shutting down your brilliant mind, ignoring the patterns that you see or giving up on improving the world. But it is about being able and willing to see (and feel) every aspect of the whole simultaneously. Have all the *opinions* you want. But remember, you are not your *opinions*. You are so much more. You are a scientist of the heart, here to contribute your part to the future of humanity by seeing the small and the big picture, all at once.

Questions for Contemplation

• Where are you being too hard on yourself? How can you be more gentle?
• Where do you actually have an opinion, but are afraid of sharing it? Where in your life could you use a backbone?

- Where do you tend to be hard on others? Are your strong opinions getting in the way of your relationships? Do you ever get caught up in defending your opinions, or trying to convert people to see things your way?
- Who is a person you admire for his or her *Farsightedness*, or capacity to see the big picture?
- What does *Omniscience* mean to you?
- Find the opposite of a strong *opinion* of yours. Sincerely look for evidence to prove this contrasting viewpoint. Stay open to what you learn.

INTEGRITY

The secret of the Gift of Integrity is to be able to hold your own space without reacting to your judgments or self-judgments.

Gift: Integrity
Shadow: Judgment
Siddhi: Perfection
Programming Partner: 17

~ Richard Rudd

My Wisdom Story

From a young age, I knew something was wrong with the way women were treated in my society. My father talked down to my mother, and she let him. Then she'd fret and complain behind his back. But she never spoke up for herself, and encouraged the same sense of *inferiority* in me.

In my teens, I became angry. I saw her life as sad and pathetic, and promised myself I'd never be an oppressed woman. So I rejected all things 'mother.' I spoke my mind, broke the rules and took on the world. I became an independent, staunch feminist, refusing to be patronized. It got to a point where my father threatened to disown me. My mother tried to calm the waters, but deep down she felt ashamed of her unruly daughter.

I left the country and built a new life as an activist and artist. When my parents visited, I'd watch my father condescend, and my mother make nice. I felt *superior* to both of them, either rolling my eyes or flying off the handle. I didn't realize just how victimized I felt by my mother's victimization until I was invited to a friend's house to meet her parents. Like mine, they came from a traditional background. The father dominated the conversation. The mother nodded and smiled. But somehow my friend was still able to enjoy them, and herself. Her kindness, and her acceptance of their limitations, brought out the best in them.

I began to *judge myself* for having judged my mother so harshly, and for not seeing how similar to my father I'd become. Despite all we'd put her through, my mother kept treating us with respect and gentleness, never losing her temper. For the first time in my life, I saw the strength in her vulnerability. Though she could still benefit from standing up for herself, she had a capacity for compassion and compromise that I desperately needed. Thanks to her, I've devoted my life to helping people understand and work through their childhoods, so they can open their hearts and live with *Integrity*.

MY GIFT TO YOU

I am here to help you complete your childhood. It takes courage to uncover the wounds from your past. As you release yourself from the messages and modeling that no longer serve you, you will be free to see and receive the gifts from your parents, with a soft, compassionate heart. When you are truly in your *Integrity*, it won't be possible to take the *judgment*s of others personally, or to identify as a victim—of yourself or anyone else. This is not a path to be walked alone, so reach out for support. Allow a friend, therapist, mentor or spiritual counselor to accompany you as you revisit those painful experiences that hardened your heart, made you feel *inferior* or *superior*, or kept you from expressing yourself freely and connecting deeply. Over time, you will learn to judge not from the mind, but from the heart.

QUESTIONS FOR CONTEMPLATION

- Where do you tend to feel *inferior*, or *superior*, to others? Who are you being hard on, even if you don't like to admit it?
- Where is self-judgment most alive in your life? Who are you negatively comparing yourself to?
- In what ways does your self-judgment keep you from owning and honoring your own inner authority?
- What does *Integrity* mean to you? Name one thing you can do today to feel more in your *Integrity*.
- How can *Perfection* be an inspiration in your life, rather than a driving force to an unattainable ideal?

SENSITIVITY

The gift of sensitivity is about being highly attuned to the needs of others. In order to sense others and their needs, you must first become independent from them.

Gift: Sensitivity
Shadow: Co-Dependence
Siddhi: Sacrifice
Programming Partner: 33

~ Richard Rudd

My Wisdom Story

I was born in the old country, where men took care of the money, women took care of the children, adults took care of the elders, and God took care of all of us. Traditions and customs made up the fabric of our lives, and we didn't question them. When my girls were little, my *sensitivity* was welcome. They'd have a need, and I'd meet it. For every runny nose, I had a tissue; for every cold, hot soup; and for every tear, a bosom to cry on.

But as they grew older, and as the world changed around us, my ability to sense what they felt and needed was shrinking. I'd give them good advice, and they'd accuse me of not listening. I'd cook them a nourishing meal, and they'd say it was unhealthy. I'd arrange for them to meet a nice boy, and they'd refuse to come out of the room. I'd even pray to God that He'd protect them, and they'd challenge He even existed. When they moved out, I called them every day. They called me *co-dependent*, saying they didn't want my worry. No matter how hard I tried to love them and be a good mother, no matter how often I told them how much I suffered in their absence, it didn't work. They just distanced themselves more and called me the *needy* one.

Finally, I did the unthinkable. I turned my back on my own children. If they didn't need me, then I didn't need them! For a long time, I *isolated* myself and was miserable, sure I had failed as a mother. But eventually my friends dragged me out of the house. A class here, a walk there. Then I started having the strangest dreams where animals would come talk to me. Soon, to my shock, the spirits of dead relatives and friends started showing up in my living room, bringing messages for me to pass along.

Word got out about my extrasensory gifts. Friends and neighbors started coming to me with their depressed pets, wilting plants, and unresolved grief. I became quite a phenomenon in the neighborhood. Even my girls were intrigued. Now they come over all the time. I'm having so much fun with my own surprising life that I let them have fun with theirs, in their own way. They even eat my food, and take my advice now and then, when they ask for it!

MY GIFT TO YOU

I am here to celebrate your *Sensitivity*, and all of the ways that you are attuned to the feelings and needs of the people in your life. Being of service is a wonderful thing. That said, when you offer your support, make sure that you are coming from a good place. Make sure you are happy with your own life, and that you are not just trying to get your own needs met by meeting the needs of others. I can guarantee you, people can smell hidden agendas. If you are isolating yourself because of hurt feelings, it's time to reach out for support. Your heart is too big and beautiful to close off for too long.

Questions for Contemplation

- Are you sacrificing too much because of your need to be needed?
- What signals does your body give you when you've been giving too much?
- Are you denying a real need of yours, because depending on another feels scary?
- Do you *isolate* yourself, and then resent people for not supporting you?
- Are you clinging to your independence? What are you afraid might happen if you let yourself *need* someone, or truly lean on them?
- How can you find a balance between caring for yourself and caring for others? What is healthy *Sensitivity*? Healthy *Sacrifice*?

SELF-ASSURANCE

With Self-Assurance must come a profound surrender to life in every moment. As you begin to accept that life has its own plans and flow, you also begin to stop interfering with the process at a mental level.

Gift: Self-assurance
Shadow: Superficiality
Siddhi: Presence
Programming Partner: 34

~ Richard Rudd

MY WISDOM STORY

Ever since I could hold a bow in my hand, I envisioned my career as a violinist. When other children played in the grass, I played my scales. My mind was constantly thinking about the future, planning my next piece, where I'd play, and whom I'd impress. Once I began performing, my mind was consumed with either obsessions about the next performance, or agonizing regrets over the last one.

While my music moved people to tears, it just kept me moving. I was always on my way from here to there, living on airplanes and stages. I knew the music so well I didn't even have to listen. I could worry about my next flight without missing a note. Sometimes after a concert, surrounded by fans, my eyes would glaze over as if I were *absent*. But most of the time, I was as *hectic* as a hive-less bee— constantly checking, calling, texting, practicing, scheduling, traveling, performing, and traveling again. I was lost in a life of success and *Superficiality*.

Until one day, I was stranded in an airport, with thousands of people waiting for me in another city, all because of a lousy storm. In a rage, I roared, throwing my briefcase onto the floor and sending hundreds of loose sheets of music into the air. The strangest thing happened as they cascaded like snowflakes in the room. I started laughing hysterically. Soon the people around me joined in. Before I knew it, I picked up my violin and started playing... just for fun. It felt like a symphony of Angels were playing through my instrument. Tears of joy streamed down my face. I had never been so present. The spirits of everyone were lifted. And from that moment on, I knew that everything was going to be okay.

MY GIFT TO YOU

I come to bring you great relief. Your mind may be busy telling you what to do. That's okay. But for this moment, I invite you to smile tenderly at your sweet worried mind, and know that everything is going to be all right. Right now, there is nothing to do. Nothing to make happen. Nothing to worry about. Nothing to regret. Not in this moment. Just take a deep breath and know that your life is in the hands of something far greater than you could ever imagine. Even if you can't feel at One with this moment, you are absolutely here, right now. I promise you. Rejoice in the wonder of *Presence*. And genuine *Self-Assurance* will be your reward.

QUESTIONS FOR CONTEMPLATION

• Do you feel *absent* from your life? Like you're going through the motions, but you're not really there?

- Does it feel impossible for you to slow down? Are you afraid of what might happen, or what you might feel, if you dropped all of that *hectic* activity?
- In what situations (and with whom) do you find it easy to be *present*? Which are more challenging?
- Spend a few minutes in front of a mirror. Look in your eyes. Is anyone home? See if you can become even more present. Can you find a way to relax? Notice the thoughts and feelings that arise as you look into your eyes. Write what you learn from this experience in your journal.

AUTHORITY

Ultimately, the only ones who will be given positions of control will be those who have given up being in control.

Gift: Authority
Shadow: Control
Siddhi: Valor
Programming Partner: 48

~ Richard Rudd

MY WISDOM STORY

I was a trust fund baby. While my dad disappeared behind closed doors with business moguls and ruled the world, my mother ruled the household—with her perfectly manicured nails and social graces. As they raised me, they were *controlling* and critical, and I was *submissive*. I cringed at the way they treated our servants, whom I suspected secretly despised my parents as much as I did.

The moment I got my driver's license, I grabbed some cash and bolted, leaving my parents and my trust fund in the dust. I had no plan, no college education. All I cared about was being free of their stuffy, oppressive world. So I worked odd jobs, went with the flow and reveled in the fact that I no longer represented the imperious elite.

But when my financial cushion ran out, so did my sense of adventure. Too humiliated to beg my parents to take me back, I lived in my car behind our house, eating the food that was thrown away. One of the servants found me there and insisted on taking me in. Her family had almost nothing, but gave me everything. I was grateful, and humbled. I realized how bitter and selfish I'd become, how deeply I resented my parents for their narrowness and selfishness, at society for ignoring the needy, and more importantly, at myself, for being too weak and pathetic to help myself, much less anyone else. I'd become as obsessed about money as my father, and as disconnected from the real world as my mother. If I truly wanted my life to be useful, I'd have to take responsibility for it.

From that point on, my heart took over. I became driven by a deep desire to give back to this family and to serve those in need. I got my act together, re-engaged with the world, and eventually reconciled with my parents. Instead of rejecting their resources, I inspired them to recognize the humanity of the people who worked for them. My parents are now the biggest financial supporters of my efforts to give homes to the homeless, bring gardens to food deserts, and represent people whose voices have not been heard. The more my heart opens, the more loyalty I inspire, in the most unlikely places.

MY GIFT TO YOU

I come to share that true power has nothing to do with money or *control*. True power is about speaking and acting from the heart, and grounding all that you do in a deep desire to serve. Becoming the true *Authority* in your own life requires both that you surrender, and that you rise up to meet whatever life brings your way, with enthusiasm, gratitude and a deep sense of responsibility. You will know that you are owning your *Authority* when you inspire loyalty and connectivity wherever you go. When everyone you represent— no matter what role they play, feels empowered, impassioned and respected. It is time to listen deeply to the will of the groups in your life, and act sincerely on their behalf. It is time to become the trustworthy person I know you can be.

QUESTIONS FOR CONTEMPLATION

- Where in your life do you feel *controlled?*
- How might the fear of being *controlled* be running your life, or influencing the decisions you make?
- Are you so afraid of misusing your power that you're not using it at all?
- In what relationships do you tend to be *controlling? Submissive?*
- Think back to your best relationships. What were the conditions that made you feel safe enough to surrender? To own your *Authority?*
- Where in your life can you surrender even more?

GRACIOUSNESS

Graciousness means that you act with grace and consideration in everything you do.

Gift: Graciousness
Shadow: Dishonor
Siddhi: Grace
Programming Partner: 47

~ Richard Rudd

My Wisdom Story

I was born into a well-respected family that cared a great deal about its reputation. But beneath the veneer, there was terrible dysfunction. When my body began to change into a beautiful young woman's body, an admired family member abused me sexually. I felt too afraid and ashamed to tell anyone what was happening. Instead, I tried desperately not to feel. Whenever a forbidden feeling arose in my heart, I'd throw myself on the floor and pray that God would make me good and pious. Because I showed such unusual religious fervor for a young girl, I was sent to a secluded monastery to live a modest life of study and prayer.

Relieved to be in a safe place, I gladly renounced all material things, took a vow of celibacy and dedicated my life to selflessness. To all at the monastery, I was a *proper*, calm and balanced woman, and a keen listener. But on the inside, I often seethed with *inappropriate* feelings that I couldn't bear to accept, much less express. I distrusted my pain, rejected my beauty, hated my needs and judged my desires. I couldn't say 'no' to requests for support, even when I was sick. I felt disgust at even the tiniest bit of passion, anger or sexual feelings within me.

One day, during a prayer group, a sister bravely shared about an experience of having been raped as a child. In the midst of her sharing, my body was hit by a tidal wave of memories, humiliation and shame. Instead of looking up to God and praying for the feelings to go away, I buried my head in my hands and sobbed. For the first time in my life, I shared about what had happened to me. I hid nothing from anyone, not even myself. As the pain, shame and loneliness of my past erupted out of my throat, I felt a kind of light and love descend into my chest, one I'd never experienced in all of my days of prayer. And when I opened my eyes, I was met with such love, compassion and respect that it felt like the entire cosmos was singing. Now I regard myself as deeply as I regard others. I no longer need to hide my beauty, *dishonor* my boundaries or withhold my feelings to engage *graciously* with the world.

MY GIFT TO YOU

I have come to tell you that there is nothing in you that is unworthy of love, or of reverence. The very things you think you should hide or get rid of are exactly what need to be seen, felt and expressed. Push nothing away. *Transparency* is the ultimate path towards *Grace*. Be unwaveringly *gracious* towards every part of yourself—every feeling, every painful experience. By honoring all that is within you, you will experience the poetry and music of even the most agonizing moments. You will naturally find yourself being *gracious* towards others, touching their emotions, hearts and souls with the *milk of human kindness*. And they will bloom in your presence.

At your core, you are a gloriously unique manifestation of *Grace*. Honor your suffering and you will discover your gift to the world.

QUESTIONS FOR CONTEMPLATION

- Are there ways that you *dishonor* yourself, or others?
- On the outside, do you appear kind, balanced, and a good listener, but inside, do you feel angry, resentful or full of forbidden desire?
- Have you ever held so much inside that you exploded? What were the consequences to yourself and those around you?
- Think of a part of you (a feeling or experience) that you reject as bad or *inappropriate*. How can you embrace it?
- How can you bring more *Graciousness* into your life?

SIMPLICITY

If you love simplicity, you will manifest it around you.

Gift: Simplicity
Shadow: Complexity
Siddhi: Quintessence
Programming Partner: 43

~ Richard Rudd

My Wisdom Story

My parents were servants of the upper class. To survive, they learned to be invisible and quiet. But not me. My mother said I was born with the urge to speak my mind. And nothing made me more uncomfortable than silence. So I made it my business to fill up my mind so I could fill up the holes in the conversation.

As a young woman, my mind raced with knowledge, facts, quotes and theories, and my mouth spouted out complicated explanations for just about everything. I offered the Truth wherever I went. And I assumed everyone knew what I meant, like they were inside my head. I had no idea that I often said the wrong thing at the wrong time, or that no one felt they could get a straight answer out of me.

Until once, a cousin of mine got honest. She said she was tired of being talked at, that what I said was so scattered and *fragmented* she could barely understand me. She said that my words were actually hurting people. I felt shocked, and ashamed.

But I also woke up. And I started listening. For the first time in my life, I slowed down enough to hear my parents' story, and just how painfully silenced they'd been their whole lives. I also realized that deep down their pain and anger lived in me. All that time, I'd been carrying around a fear of being silenced, and of being seen as *dumb* and ignorant.

Now there are few things I love more than silence and *Simplicity*. My home is as uncluttered as my mind. Problems naturally dissolve when I'm around. Things that seem difficult become easy. When I listen, I listen deeply, and to all of life. I prefer to go days without talking. But when I do use my voice, I wait for the right moment, get to the point and speak from the heart.

MY GIFT TO YOU

Do you want to be happy? I'm here to encourage you to keep it simple and to slow it all down. You don't have to solve every problem. Find the clutter in your mind and environment, and then let it all go. Notice how much more relaxed your body becomes when you release yourself from having to figure it all out. I invite you to trust that life has its own way of dissolving knots. Imagine yourself up above your life, looking down. How many of the things you fret about truly need fretting? Drop into a deeper stillness. Go for a walk. Smell the flowers. Listen to the breeze. And while you listen, breathe deep into your belly, and remind yourself that you don't have to have it all sorted out in your head. Try accepting the moment exactly as it is… and see what happens. Beneath what you think… is what you truly know. Let your knowing, gentle heart lead the way towards luscious *Simplicity*.

QUESTIONS FOR CONTEMPLATION

- Do you tend to get tongue-tied out of fear, talk too much, or say the wrong thing?

- Have you learned to remain silent, even though you have something to say? Do you rarely share what you're truly feeling and thinking?

- Where are you making your life more complicated than it needs to be? Where is your life calling out for greater *Simplicity*?

- Pick an area of your life in need of decluttering. Commit to releasing something (a thought, feeling, object, relationship) this week.

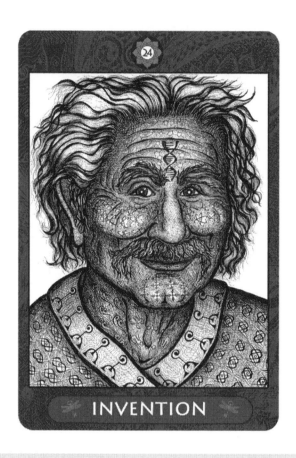

INVENTION

The 24th Gift is truly magical and contains the secret to genius. Genius is far more than lateral thinking—it is the ability to make quantum leaps.

Gift: Invention
Shadow: Addiction
Siddhi: Silence
Programming Partner: 44

~ Richard Rudd

MY WISDOM STORY

I was a sensitive boy with an insatiably curious mind. With a deep love of logic and learning, my parents encouraged me to study everything from math, to chemistry, to astrophysics. My unusual gifts for predicting patterns and solving problems were discovered by my professors, and eventually the world.

By the time I was a young adult, many people counted on my mind to answer some of the most difficult questions about our shared future. As the pressure amped up, there was less room for error, for feelings, free time, or the present moment. Once, I was working on a problem, and my mind spun round and round. My body got tight, and I started to panic. I was *frozen*. Not knowing how to cope with the awful sense of failure and emptiness I felt, I grabbed a glass of wine, which helped my mind and body to relax. And mysteriously, the breakthrough I'd been waiting for spontaneously appeared.

After that, any time I couldn't solve a problem, or felt *anxious*, I drank. The bigger the problem, the more I drank. It took a deep depression and several crises for me to recognize my *addiction* and accept the truth: there was no escape, nowhere to go. Nothing in the outside world could ever end the pain, anxiety and emptiness I was so desperately trying to avoid.

So I turned the intelligence of my mind inward. I used my mind to watch itself, and I got so good at recognizing its patterns and repetitive loops that just naturally they began to loosen their hold. Whenever I bumped up against my ignorance, suffering or an unknown, instead of pushing against it or numbing out, I dropped in. Now I think in spirals, not loops. I welcome the unknown, rejoice in life's mysteries, and have come to cherish creative *Invention* and innovation above solving problems—although my knack for solving problems continues to expand. My most creative moments and breakthrough insights often happen when I'm relaxing, dreaming or doing nothing at all. I'm constantly surprised by how art, music, philosophy, mythology and psychology relate to all that I do.

MY GIFT TO YOU

I'm here to tell you that *addiction* is not only about what you do, but how you think. And especially how you think during those moments in your life where you bump against the unknown, your own ignorance, a deafening *silence* and an inner emptiness. There are whole worlds of possibility in the space between thoughts, sounds, even between your impulses and cravings. One of the most difficult, yet most rewarding things you can do in life is to embrace those gaps in your awareness. Don't push your anxiety away. Don't fill in those holes. As you make peace with emptiness and befriend uncertainty, your talent for *Invention,* creative thinking and living will flourish.

QUESTIONS FOR CONTEMPLATION

- How do you cope with moments of emptiness or anxiety?
- What role has *addiction* played in your life? Have you used substances, behaviors or activities to numb yourself or fill a hole?
- Today, pay attention to an arising feeling of emptiness. Before reaching for that cookie, cup of coffee, glass of beer, or the television remote, phone or computer, take a 3-minute pause to breathe, and see what happens.
- Where in your life do you feel innovative?
- Is there something new that wants to be born in you?
- Find one simple way to cultivate more inner and outer *Silence* in your life?

ACCEPTANCE

The path of love is the path of acceptance. In order to accept something about yourself, and especially something uncomfortable, it must first be recognized.

Gift: Acceptance
Shadow: Constriction
Siddhi: Universal Love
Programming Partner: 46

~ Richard Rudd

MY WISDOM STORY

I grew up in a strict household, where boys were expected to be strong. Even when my beloved older brother died from an illness, I wasn't allowed to cry. I took all of the pain and vulnerability inside of me and buried it deep within. I married at a young age to a kind, sensitive woman who took care of our home and gave me two sons. I provided for my family, but I was emotionally *ignorant* and *constricted*. There were times my wife would ask me if I was happy. Not knowing what to say, I'd tell her I was fine.

Until the day my first-born son died. My wife's broken heart flowed like a river, while mine turned to ice. I wouldn't allow his name to be spoken and forced my wife to get rid of anything that reminded me of our son. Then I became obsessed with things. My house. My money. My wife. My child. They were all mine. I forbade my wife and youngest son from leaving the house. If they showed signs of emotional weakness, I became *cold* or exploded with rage. At times I could barely breathe. I was engulfed by a fear so primal it pervaded every moment of every day. I hated that fear, and lashed out at anyone who reminded me of it. I was completely unreachable.

It wasn't until I discovered that my wife had kept a picture of our first-born, and saw my son's terror as I raised my hand to strike her, that I collapsed onto the floor, shaking like a leaf. Though I didn't deserve it, my wife and son held me until my tears thawed out my heart. My breath deepened. My body gave way to the grief of my entire life. Finally, a love, lightness—and softness—came over me, my wife and son, that we had never known.

This was many years ago, but it marked the beginning of a blessed and joyous family life, filled with love poems, whirling dances and mystical celebrations. Look into my eyes, and you will feel the love that comes from *accepting*—and being *accepted* in—one's darkest wounds.

My Gift to You

When I look into your eyes, I see innocence and trustworthiness. A deep optimism that remains untouched—no matter what has happened in your life. I know from experience just how difficult it can be to experience true *Acceptance*—of yourself, of another. Like me, you will be tested in this life. But I am here to reassure you that if you commit yourself to embracing your deepest wounds, no matter how deep and painful they are, you will find that there is no wound in this whole world that you cannot bear, or embrace. Worries and grudges will naturally slip away. And wherever you go, you will know, in the depths of your heart, that you belong. I come to bathe you in the warmth of unconditional and *Universal Love*. You are so worthy.

QUESTIONS FOR CONTEMPLATION

- What experience from your past have you not yet fully accepted?
- What wound are you refusing to feel? How can you give expression to that wound? To a person? In a poem?
- Have you ever opened up to your pain and discovered a greater capacity for love, and a deeper connection with the world?
- When have you experienced *Universal Love*? How did it feel?
- If you can feel that you carry a very big wound, I invite you to seek support from someone (a counselor, therapist, or spiritual guide) who can hold your hand as you move towards *Acceptance*, and liberate your heart.

ARTFULNESS

The 26th Gift celebrates your ego without self-judgment and in full awareness.

Gift: Artfulness
Shadow: Pride
Siddhi: Invisibility
Programming Partner: 45

~ Richard Rudd

My Wisdom Story

My father was a conventional, hard-working man. "No pain, no gain," he always said. He never understood my acting ambitions, so I went on a mission to prove him wrong and make him—and myself—*proud*. I would become a famous, respected actor. If I had to kiss up to a producer, seduce my fans, or publicly criticize a competitor, so be it. My 'take no prisoners' strategy worked. I climbed up the ladder of fame with the sheer force of my will. I was in every blockbuster, *boasting* every chance I got. My public relations team milked my celebrity and dealt with the fallout, while I tracked my popularity and courted my fans. I was addicted to stress. I couldn't relax, not for a single moment, until my immune system crashed.

As I watched my celebrity fade along with my physical strength, I became aware of just how terrified I'd always been of disappearing, of discovering that my life didn't matter. I started feeling pangs of guilt for all of the ways I had *manipulated* and disrespected people who had seemed weak and vulnerable to me. I started questioning the dreams I always believed were mine, and everything I had learned about success.

Thanks to my body, I was forced to stop imposing my will on the world, and to start listening within. Over time, I felt calmer, and my heart grew warmer. My immune system strengthened as a new intention grew inside of me. I wanted to serve the world through my art, not just prove my worth. So I began writing plays for smaller stages—plays about love, life, humility and the human experience. My passion for the creative process just naturally drew the attention of the right people. For the first time in my life, it felt like magic was at work. I still love the spotlight, but now I know I am no longer selling myself. I am selling Love.

MY GIFT TO YOU

I am here to recognize the *Artfulness* in you. I come when it is time for you to 'market' from the heart. What is the essential message you want to share with the world? How does your Love long to be expressed? What is the deeper intention behind your offerings? When you share a genuine gift with the world, know that you are turning an ability to manipulate out of fear into an ability to 'manipulate' the world into becoming a more caring, inspiring place. Remember that Intention and Will are not the same thing. Let go of thinking that you can only achieve your goals through willpower, or by giving your mind the reigns. Half the time, your mind doesn't even know what you want. I'm asking you to reach deeper. And while you're reaching, stop judging your *pride* and ego. Embrace and celebrate them for their ability to make dreams come true.

Questions for Contemplation

- How does *Pride* express itself in your life? Out in the open? Beneath the surface? Be honest.
- When growing up, what did you learn about 'selling yourself,' or about what it takes to be a 'success'? Were you taught that if you don't use your willpower to make something happen, it won't?
- Where might you be pushing too hard with your will?
- Think of a time that you experienced a magical synchronicity in relation to a creative process. What attitude were you holding at the time?
- What does living an *Artful* life mean to you?
- Find a simple way to open up to more magic and ease in your life.

ALTRUISM

To give to others simply for the sake of giving
activates healthy currents deep within your body.

Gift: Altruism
Shadow: Selfishness
Siddhi: Selflessness
Programming Partner: 28

~ Richard Rudd

MY WISDOM STORY

My people looked down upon *selfishness*. Status and respect were earned through generous giving and personal sacrifice, not through *self-centered* accumulating and individual achievement. From the moment I could hold something in my hands, I learned to give it away. On birthdays, I gave gifts to my guests. When participating in ceremony, I gave gifts to my teacher and those around me. When I became a young woman, I served my family willingly and without complaint. But there were times when I was expected to give, and I felt taken advantage of and disrespected. Even though I felt angry and resentful inside, I gave anyway. Because that's what good community members did. Sometimes I found myself giving because I secretly wanted something from someone else—their respect, their love, their admiration, their gratitude.

Once, I worked for several days preparing a meal for the whole village, when what I really wanted to be doing was swimming in the river with my brothers. My *self-sacrifice* seemed to go unnoticed and unappreciated. Without realizing it, I pounded my frustrations into the tortillas that I made. When some of the villagers got ill after the meal, I felt just horrible. As I was about to confess to the elders that my self-centered heart had poisoned the food, my grandmother—a master gardener—stood up and told the community that she hadn't properly tended to the corn, and that the belly aches were her fault. Then she winked at me and pointed me in the direction of the river. That evening, as I floated and looked up at the moon, I realized that my grandmother had taught me the meaning of true *Altruism*.

MY GIFT TO YOU

It is time to look honestly at your relationship to giving. Are you giving from your heart, or are you giving away your power? Are you giving without attachment, or with a hidden agenda? What did you learn during the first seven years of your life about *selfishness* and *Selflessness*? I ask you to be intuitive in your giving. Give to causes and to people who are fertile, who can make use of the gifts they receive. If you are feeling angry or resentful, do not give. Not yet. Wait until your heart opens. Practice random acts of kindness whenever possible. And your sincere *Altruism* will bring more joy and abundance into your life than you can possibly imagine.

QUESTIONS FOR CONTEMPLATION

• Where are you sacrificing yourself in ways that aren't healthy for you? Where are you giving with strings?

- Have you ever given too much of yourself and then resented it later? How can you better care for yourself so you can give from a full cup?
- Where and with whom do you find it most difficult to set healthy limits?
- Where and with whom do you tend towards *selfishness*?
- If you weren't feeling so guilty, what might you do differently? Or do less of?
- When have you felt the most *Selfless* in your actions?
- What are you feeling genuinely grateful for right now? Write it in your journal.
- Do something nice for someone today—without them knowing it. It's good for your health.

TOTALITY

There is a deep sense of thrill that comes as you progressively face your inner demons.

Gift: Totality
Shadow: Purposelessness
Siddhi: Immortality
Programming Partner: 27

~ Richard Rudd

MY WISDOM STORY

I was a sensitive, fearful child. I looked around me and saw all that could go wrong. I could lose someone I loved. An earthquake could hit. A bomb could go off. I could fall and hurt myself. I could get sick. My heart could break. Wherever I looked, I felt unsafe.

As I grew older, I became obsessed with life, or rather, with avoiding death. At first I focused on safety and survival. I worked hard to stay healthy, to make money, to build a home, and to become a pious member of the community. Though I seemed happy and at ease to others, I felt *hollow* inside. Deep down, I knew I was meant to do more with my life. But I was afraid to do it. I was waiting for a readiness that never seemed to come.

The quality of my fears began to change. I became less worried about not making a living, and more worried about having no reason to live. I began experiencing night terrors. As soon as my head hit the pillow, I was chased down, struck by gremlins and obliterated by natural disasters. I started avoiding sleep, too afraid to close my eyes. Instead, wide-eyed and reckless, I hurled myself into activity after activity, determined to fill up my life with meaning and a sense of security. If I could only take more risks, or do more, or do it faster, I thought.

So I bought a bicycle and tore down the street without a helmet. My *gambling* behavior landed me in the hospital. For months, I was forced to be still, with eyes closed and nothing but my inner demons to keep me company. As I was lying there, immobilized, I had no choice but to face the multitude of fears I had been trying to escape ever since I was a child. My fear of pain, of pleasure, of the past, of the future, of failure, of success, of life, of death, of non-existence, of *purposelessness*. It wasn't until I gave myself fully to the fear that the strangest thing happened. All of my senses heightened, an inexplicable sense of aliveness welled up in my heart, and I was overcome by the eternal nature of my human spirit.

From that moment on, I've trusted life and committed myself unconditionally to whatever it's brought me.

MY GIFT TO YOU

It is time to stop postponing your life, and to embrace the entirety of it—the pain as much as the pleasure. I bring you the Gift of *Totality*. I ask you to surrender yourself entirely to Life's mystery. In this moment, close your eyes. Be still. Listen with ever-widening ears. If possible, move willingly towards the dark. You will soon discover that your demons are only divine messengers in disguise. As you whole-heartedly make friends with adversity, you will find yourself feeling increasingly unfettered. When you are no longer afraid of death, you will finally be free to do what you've come here to do—leave an eternal mark on this planet with the golden ink of your heart. To be alive is to be here. Now. Fully. That is all.

QUESTIONS FOR CONTEMPLATION

- Is there an inner demon you have been refusing to face?
- Are you constantly in motion?
- Do you engage in risky behavior in order to escape from how you feel inside?
- Are you terrified of being still? What are you scared of?
- Are you forever looking for your life purpose? Do you know what it is, but can never follow through?
- When was the last time you felt deeply aligned with your Purpose? Or connected to the *Totality* of existence?
- Write your own eulogy. Find a creative way to honor your own *Immortality.* Share what you write with someone you love.

COMMITMENT

A clear decision is felt as a quiet and powerful warmth that courses through your whole being.

Gift: Commitment
Shadow: Half-heartedness
Siddhi: Devotion
Programming Partner: 30

~ Richard Rudd

My Wisdom Story

My parents always called me 'the free bird.' That was their sweet way of saying I was an *unreliable* flake. I was always flitting about, from romance to romance, place to place, career to career. Always starting what I couldn't finish. So when I finally found social work, and a wonderful organization that suited me well, everyone was thrilled, including me.

I worked there for years. I grew within the organization, loved the population, and felt my life was meaningful. But after 7 years, I found myself *over-committed*, burned out and disengaged. My heart yearned to be somewhere else, doing something more creative. I wanted more space in my life for intimacy. My colleagues and staff had no idea how *half-hearted* I'd become about the job. I was lying to them, and I was lying to myself.

I was also terrified of leaving. They needed me, and I certainly didn't want to risk quitting, or failing, or seeming unreliable. So I waited, and waited. Each time someone dared to quit the agency to go after a dream, I felt jealous, like I was on the sidelines launching other people's happiness, while watching mine drift farther and farther away. To top it off, I felt even more trapped. Without me, who would train the new people?

Finally, just as I spilled 16 ounces of coffee all over the giant pile of paperwork on my desk, it hit me. The timing would never feel right. I could never guarantee that my next step would be a success. And I had no control over what others thought of me. Suddenly, a warmth ran through my body, and I knew what I had to do. The following day I gave notice. While I will always cherish my time working in that organization, I have not looked back. Not once. I have no regrets.

My Gift to You

I am here to give you permission to say YES to life. To trust it fully. It is time to hold nothing back. Don't worry about what others think or expect from you. Beware of giving your power away to a teacher, guru or a system. Fly brave and blind as you embark on your path. And remember, few things are less healthy for you than *half-heartedness*. So whether you are succeeding or failing, do it with a full heart. Stand by your decisions. Trust your in-the-moment guidance. Honor the stream of your experiences and relationships until each cycle reaches its natural completion. Do these things, and there will be no need to worry about the future, for the seed of your dreams lives in the heart of your *Commitment*. It's all about the journey.

Questions for Contemplation

- Where in your life are you *over-committed*?

- Where do you feel like a slave, or like you're being taken advantage of, or abused?

- What in your life (a job, relationship, way of being) needs to come to an end?

- What do you fear might happen if you honor and follow through with what you know to be true?

- Where are you lacking *Commitment*? Where are you living *half-heartedly*? Are you saying yes, but then not following through? Is there a frustration, fear or anger behind your seeming flakiness that you haven't fully owned?

- How can you more deeply *commit* to the needs of your soul?

- Think of a time in your life when you experienced *Devotion*.

- Where in your life today are you satisfied with your level of *Commitment*? Honor these experiences in your journal.

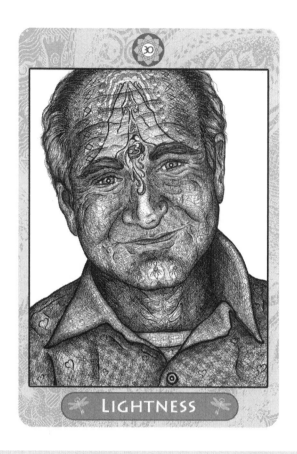

LIGHTNESS

As every human being learns, the cycle of desire is eternal.

Gift: Lightness
Shadow: Desire
Siddhi: Rapture
Programming Partner: 29

~ Richard Rudd

MY WISDOM STORY

I was said to have shot out of my mother's womb like a rocket, and then nursed like a baby whale. As soon as I could talk, I made people laugh. And as soon as I could walk, I ran everywhere I wasn't supposed to go. I was on a mission to experience every single part of life. So I gobbled it up throughout my teens, and found myself becoming a young actor. I wanted to experience the sound of applause. I loved being able to be anyone and try anything my mind could dream up. Soon I *desired* the experience of being rich and famous. And so I tried that for a long time. I threw my money around like gum wrappers and chewed up my fans like chips.

But those *flippant* times only made me feel empty and alone. My sensitive soul hungered for something different, and deeper. I wanted to use every single one of my gifts, so that I could have an even bigger impact. Soon I was popular all over the world. But no matter how huge or demanding my achievements were, I still wanted more.

For a while I thought I'd be happy if I could just learn to completely trust my instincts. When I mastered that, all I wanted was for my performances to lift the spirit of all of humanity. But I couldn't escape that awful feeling of wanting more. Until the fire in me all but burned out. I became depressed, and *over-serious*. My only *desire* was to end *desire*.

That is when I discovered Buddhism, and meditated for hours in order to become One with everything, and finally transcend my never-ending ache. But soon I realized even that was a *desire*. No matter what I did, the *desire* would not go away.

The moment I faced my *desire*, admitted defeat, and accepted that it wasn't going to go away, things started to change. I started to lighten up. But not in an ungrounded way. I genuinely stopped trying to control my life. I surrendered totally to all of it, even the most painful parts, including my utter helplessness in relation to my own *desires*, and the inevitable disappointments that followed. I was finally free.

MY GIFT TO YOU

I bring good and bad news. The bad: You are not in control of your destiny, and you are never going to get rid of your *desire*. The good: Accepting this bad news will free you to trust in life. It's time to fully feel your *desires*, and to realize that feeling them doesn't mean acting on them indiscriminately, or repressing them. You can welcome a *desire* into your home without allowing it to control your life. Being human is quite a trip, and Life is quite a game. A comedy and tragedy all at once. You might as well enjoy the ride. Keep a sense of humor. Do not pretend to live lightly. Embrace and emanate a true *Lightness* of being. With such an attitude, you won't need to fear your feelings, no matter how painful. A *Lightness* will burn so bright in you, it'll beam out of your eyes, no matter what is happening.

QUESTIONS FOR CONTEMPLATION

- Where are you taking life *too seriously?*
- Is your strict adherence to certain principles preventing you from exploring your true passions? Is it possible that some of the *desires* you've been rejecting aren't as bad, dangerous or unhealthy as you've come to believe?
- Are your *desires* in control of you? Are you overindulging in what feels good, without taking responsibility for the consequences?
- Think of someone who for you embodies true *Lightness* of Being.
- Have you ever experienced true *Rapture?* Was it wonderful, scary, enlightening?

LEADERSHIP

If you want to really see the nature of success on the material plane, then the heart represents the cutting edge today.

Gift: Leadership
Shadow: Arrogance
Siddhi: Humility
Programming Partner: 41

~ Richard Rudd

My Wisdom Story

My father and his father preserved the peaceful traditions of my people, stayed close to the land and led through their presence, not their words. But when I was young, I was kidnapped by the State and forced into a boarding school run by the Church. They taught me that my people were heathens, and that our way of life was no good.

Over time, as my spirit broke, I *deferred* my power to the teachers and eventually forgot the ways of my people. I thought, spoke and acted like the white man. Years later, when I returned to my village, I looked upon my people *scornfully* and with pity. I *arrogantly* believed that if they wanted to survive and put an end to their suffering, they needed to drop the old ways and join the rest of the world. I addressed my people, infusing my speech with feigned humility and native phrases. I spun a tale of future promise and prosperity, if only they would follow me.

As I spoke, I felt confident and special. My father and grandfather just sat in silence. When it came time for my people to follow me out of the reservation and into the future, no one moved. Instead, they looked to my father and grandfather for guidance—

two men who had no interest in arguing or imposing their agenda on anyone.

As my grandfather spoke on behalf of the community, in simple yet potent words, I was hit by a deluge of pain and humility. I hadn't scratched the surface of my people's reality, or my own suffering. Why on earth would they want to follow me? I went on to spend years listening to and recording the stories of my people— the elders, the people who had also been torn from their homes and put in boarding schools, the women, the children. It wasn't until many years later, long after I had given up on wanting to be a leader, that I found myself sharing these stories in a way that moved the hearts of the white man, and inspired my people to participate in their own liberation.

My Gift to You

I come to free you from your own conditioning, and to make you aware of just how much you still care about what others think. Be honest with yourself. Where—and with whom—are you being *arrogant?* How are you still spinning the truth in order to be admired, respected or to gain more power? It is through wizening up to these tendencies, no matter how subtle, that your true capacity for *Leadership* is born. It is time to recognize the limitations of your own intellect. True *Leadership* does not require a superior mind, or the recognition that you are a Leader. It doesn't require that you always know what you're going to say. It is not even about finding and projecting your own voice. It is about listening deeply to others and using your voice to represent theirs. No matter what you do, whether you are speaking, writing or creating, do it with *Humility* and heart.

QUESTIONS FOR CONTEMPLATION

- Do you ever put yourself down to avoid seeming *arrogant*?
- Do you ever defer your power to others?
- Do you ever find yourself being arrogant? In what situations? What feelings are underneath the *arrogance*?
- In what areas of life are you a leader? Have you ever been able to represent others by listening deeply and giving them a voice?
- Do you lead in the spirit of *Humility* and service?
- Think of a *leader* in your life, or in the world, for whom you have great respect. What qualities do you most appreciate in this *leader*? What is one thing you can do today to be more like this person?

PRESERVATION

As we listen to the great wisdom of our ancestors and of the indigenous tribal cultures, we will once again find our correct inner spirit.

Gift: Preservation
Shadow: Failure
Siddhi: Veneration
Programming Partner: 42

~ Richard Rudd

MY WISDOM STORY

My younger brother and I were both trained in the sacred medicine tradition. We lived side by side in the rainforest, each with our own simple camp. We always shared everything we had and served the same local community, until a foreigner came to one of my brother's ceremonies, and was so transformed by the experience that he spread the word far and wide about my brother's healing powers. Soon people started flying in from all over the world to work with my brother.

At first I was happy for him. But over time, I watched his small camp turn into a retreat center, and watched him travel to distant countries to share our medicine and tradition with strange people who knew nothing about our ways. He brought back objects and healing practices I didn't recognize. Even the way he pruned, weeded and brewed the medicine seemed new. His plants thrived in ways that made me feel uncomfortable.

A *constriction* and anger took hold of my chest. I believed this was because he was betraying our ancestors, and that it was my job to preserve the traditions. When my students showed curiosity about my brother, I acted like a true *fundamentalist*, forbidding them from visiting his Center, warning them against his tainted ways. When my brother reached out to me with gifts, I refused them. Until he gave up.

My community shrank like my heart. Slowly, my medicine began to lose its potency; my prayers stopped working; the animals stopped communicating with me. I felt *disjointed*. I was as cut off from the Great Creator as I was from my brother.

Sensing my soul's suffering, he reached out to me one last time. I was shocked to see the pain in his eyes. It had never occurred to me that his soul was also suffering. He had been missing me, my love and guidance, and he feared I had rejected and disapproved of everything he did. It was then I realized that my own fear of *failure* had blinded me to my brother's humanity. I took his hand in mine, and ever since, we've been each other's teacher, student and best friend. Our community and medicine are thriving.

MY GIFT TO YOU

This may not make sense, but it is true. When you refuse to receive, you are being selfish. If you truly long to experience success, then you must let go of the entire concept of success and *failure*. It is not your desire for money or outer recognition that you need to overcome; it is your fear of *failure*. I am here to encourage you to trust your instincts and reach beyond your comfort zone. The Gift of *Preservation* is all about preserving Life itself, not just yourself. It requires that you learn from and ground yourself in the wisdom of your ancestors. It also asks you not to be afraid to learn and invest in something new, or to receive from those who inspire you. It's time to look at your life and determine what and who are worthy of your energy, and good for the whole. See what you want to keep alive. And honor that with your whole heart.

QUESTIONS FOR CONTEMPLATION

- Where are you flourishing in your life? What (who) could use even more of your care, energy and investment?
- Where do you feel like a *failure*?
- Are there ways in which you have been isolating yourself?
- Do you tend to mistrust those who are different from you?
- Use your instincts to know who your true allies are.
- Find a place in your life where you've been resisting change. Write down what you appreciate most about how things are. Then find a way to breathe new life and Spirit into the old routine.

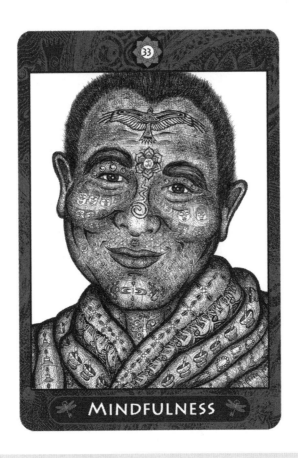

MINDFULNESS

There is no situation on earth that cannot be used as a means to raise your frequency and open your heart to your inner Divinity.

Gift: Mindfulness
Shadow: Forgetting
Siddhi: Revelation
Programming Partner: 19

~ Richard Rudd

MY WISDOM STORY

My mother was an angry woman, always *censoring* my father, claiming to help him by telling him how to be, what to do. Most of the time he just took it. But sometimes he'd explode, and it scared me. All I wanted was to get away from the tension and find peace. One day, a monk came through our town. I was only four years old, but I clung to his leg and wouldn't let go. It was like I had always known him. He asked my parents for permission to take me with him to the monastery, and they agreed—even though I could see that it broke their hearts.

I spent the next many years living in silence, living far away from people. My days were spent meditating and tending to the tasks of the monastery, and trying to forget where I came from. All I wanted was to attain liberation and leave the world of illusion. I was a *reserved* man, who most of the time felt safe, calm and at peace.

Until one week, for the first time since I was a young boy, my parents came to the monastery. My whole body recoiled, my heart raced and I felt flooded by an intensity of feelings I had long forgotten. My teacher quickly stepped in. In a stern voice, he told me to be compassionate towards my parents, and to tame my ego. In a way I'd never done before, I raised my voice in anger at my teacher, defending myself against attack, as if he were my mother, telling me what to do, how to be. And suddenly, as the heat infused my cheeks, I Remembered.

The anger I felt wasn't about my teacher, or my parents. This story I was living out, this suffering that flooded my whole body, was as old as time itself. So I watched my blood boil, and felt my heart break. Then I looked at my parents, now in old, tired bodies, and saw the pain and confusion in their eyes. That visit marked a turning point in my life, and the end of my stay at the monastery. I was ready to remember and reclaim all that I was, am and ever will be. It was time to return to the beautiful, messy world.

MY GIFT TO YOU

I am here to help you Remember. And to release you from the prison of your emotional life. Even if you want to speed up enlightenment, you can't. So give yourself plenty of permission… to think, to feel, to desire, to react, to hide. Let nothing be forbidden. All I ask is that you be *Mindful* of what you do. The first step in awakening is realizing that you've been asleep. So do not try to change your patterns or passions. Just recognize them. "Ah, there I go again." Catch yourself *forgetting* your true nature. Learn to feel increasingly comfortable with discomfort. In time, you will naturally come to realize that something more wondrous than you can imagine is looking through your eyes, thinking through your mind and living through your actions. In the end, all of Life shall remember itself through you. And all that you'll experience is the *Revelation* of the eternal Now.

QUESTIONS FOR CONTEMPLATION

- How do you avoid intimacy? Do you hide behind your work, a spiritual practice, or a philosophy?
- Do you sometimes find yourself offering unasked-for advice or criticism, or surprised by others' reactions to what you say?
- If you weren't worried about being unenlightened, what feeling, desire or need might you more easily see and own?
- Practice *Mindfulness* today. Simply watch your thoughts, impulses and actions, without trying to change, re-direct or *censor* them. Notice which ones are most difficult for you to look upon with neutral compassion.

STRENGTH

We are talking about the ability to act in harmony with natural forces—the real definition of strength.

Gift: Strength
Shadow: Force
Siddhi: Majesty
Programming Partner: 20

~ Richard Rudd

MY WISDOM STORY

I was a small and scrawny boy, bullied throughout my childhood. Raised by my parents to be humble, I allowed myself to be mistreated. Instead of speaking out, I stuffed my feelings down with food. As I grew in height and width, the teasing intensified. Once a bully taunted me with a stick. To everyone's shock, especially mine, my body lunged at him with a pure *force* I didn't know I had. Next thing I knew, he was whimpering on the ground.

Word got out at school about my physical power. I took the advice of one of my teachers who suggested I be trained in Sumo wrestling. In class, my potential was recognized quickly. I was soon moved into a training stable where every aspect of my life became highly regimented and dictated by strict tradition. My capacity for *self-effacement* was praised, and I followed all of the rules in the stable. But I found myself breaking them in the ring. I'd look into the eyes of my opponent and see the bullies from my past. Rage and the desire to humiliate would overcome me, and my timing would suffer. Sometimes I'd lose, but mostly I'd get thrown out of the game.

One day, my stable master reprimanded me for my *bullheadedness*. "I'm trying my hardest," I exclaimed. He saw right through my anger and into the deep sadness within me. Then he said something I'll never forget. "*Force* comes from the mind, but true *Strength* is rooted in the belly." Then he told me that Sumo wrestling, at its core, was meant to be an act of harmony, a sacred opportunity to embody gratitude and to purify the heart, not to obliterate enemies. The ring was there to provide me with both the freedom and the boundaries I needed. Then he instructed me to stop trying, forcing, resisting and thinking.

In the years that followed, I learned to surrender my 'self' so completely that I'm now known all over as a dancer of primal power and pure awareness. I am content beyond imagining.

MY GIFT TO YOU

I come to acknowledge your *Strength*, and to ask you to purify your heart by liberating yourself from the war in your mind. Be careful not to mistake the people around you for your enemies. Your true enemies are your own misguided thoughts, your reactive emotions and everything in you that wrestles you away from the present moment. It's time to stop trying to *force* things to go a certain way, just because your mind tells you so. Stay open to outside influence. Keep tuning into the natural world around you. Listen for the flow of life, and you shall tap into it. There is an inexhaustible reserve of inner *Strength* deep in your belly. It is greater than you can possibly imagine.

QUESTIONS FOR CONTEMPLATION

- Are you afraid of your own power?
- In what situations do you tend to hold it back?
- Did you ever learn that *force* is necessary to get what you want? How might this belief still be impacting your life?
- Have you (or others) ever been surprised by the intensity of your own impact?
- Have you ever surrendered so deeply to a physical activity, dance or movement that you lost total track of time?
- Remember a time when you experienced inner *Strength*. Where were you? What happened? How did you feel?
- Find an image that for you reflects true *Majesty*. Place it somewhere you can see it easily and often. Journal any thoughts that arise.

ADVENTURE

To live with an open heart is to live in a perpetual state of adventure.

Gift: Adventure
Shadow: Hunger
Siddhi: Boundlessness
Programming Partner: 5

~ Richard Rudd

My Wisdom Story

I was born into an entirely boring household, to dreamless parents who lived lives of complacency and drudgery. Their fear of *adventure* planted in me an unfathomable restlessness. I had no idea what I wanted, but I *hungered* for more, and I wanted it now. At first I ravaged the food on my plate. Then I *hungered* for liquor, women and money.

After years of filling my belly, bed and bank account, it was time to eat up the entire world. So I set sail for distant shores, accumulating new riches and romances. I conquered entire lands, and the people in them. I was *manic*, and so consumed with the *hunger* for progress and the chance to explore new territories that I had no idea I was exploiting them. Still, it was never enough. Each new potential land, trade and woman eventually *bored* me. I always wanted something in return, and I never got more than disappointment and anger.

One day, disgusted with the whole world, I ripped a priceless ring off of my finger and threw it at a young beggar in the street. My intention was to hurt him. But when he discovered the treasure that it was, his eyes lit up like the sun and he looked at me with such gratitude that my heart skipped a beat. I put the experience out of my mind, but then weeks later, the boy tracked me down and brought me to his humble home, to show me the relief and comfort the ring had brought to his family. I couldn't resist the power of their love.

That was the day my heart became the final frontier. From then on, the more deeply I ventured into my own heart, the more I understood the magnificence of the world. I was no longer driven by a fear of *boredom*. I was fueled by a deep love of the unknown, and the glorious world of which I was a humble part. Now I live in a constant state of *Adventure*. Whenever I have an opportunity to give something away, I give it. There is no greater fulfillment than seeing the radiant eyes of a grateful human being.

MY GIFT TO YOU

I come to make sure that the progress of your outer life isn't happening at the expense of your inner life. You will never solve your problems by stuffing yourself with experiences, people or objects. Nor will you solve your problems by starving yourself. It is time to face the *Hunger* inside of you with humility. Allow yourself to see and feel how you are held hostage by it, and how so many (if not all) of your actions arise out of this insatiable craving. Only then will you begin to feel and experience the freedom you truly seek. It is time to give unconditionally, for unconditional giving is the path to freedom, joy and *boundless Adventure*. Look out at the horizon and ask yourself, "What more can I give?"

Questions for Contemplation

- Is your life boring or lacking *Adventure*?
- Do you avoid *boredom* at all costs by keeping busy, or forever looking for that next heightened experience?
- Where is your *hunger* insatiable?
- Where are you starving yourself?
- When was the last time you felt you were on a true *Adventure*, or experienced a sense of *Boundlessness*?
- Is there an outer or inner *Adventure* calling you now?
- What would you say is your heart's cutting edge?
- Think of a simple random act of kindness you can do today. Do it. Journal what it felt like to give unconditionally.

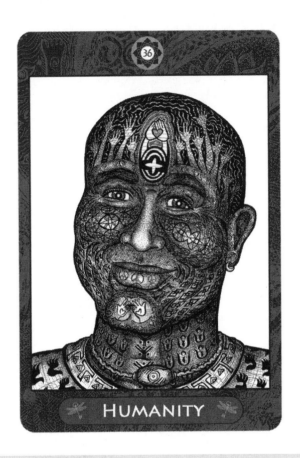

HUMANITY

The deepest role of the 36th Gift is to help humans to become human, by respecting others and by embracing your own suffering whatever it looks like, rather than being dragged down into the depths of victimhood.

Gift: Humanity
Shadow: Turbulence
Siddhi: Compassion
Programming Partner: 6

~ Richard Rudd

My Wisdom Story

The world expected my father to be a bad seed. So he became one. He cheated on my mother, had a bad temper, and created chaos wherever he went. Like many of the men in our neighborhood, he was reckless, always pushing the limit, getting into trouble and attracting *crisis* after *crisis*. He didn't mean to hurt us, which is probably why he hid so much from us, and why he begged for forgiveness when my mother and grandmother finally kicked him out.

My mother and grandmother were strong women who did their best to raise and protect me. Their task wasn't easy, given our *turbulent* neighborhood, where the police frightened us as much as the gangs. I witnessed more tragedies than a young boy ever should. I also watched the news and saw how men like my father were perceived. I promised myself I'd never be like him or cause the pain he caused.

As a teen, if I felt anger or lust, I'd go with my grandmother to church and pray for my sins to be taken away. But over time, the stress got to me, and my *nervousness* gave me ticks. Though inside I was sensitive and caring, I avoided eye contact with people and appeared shifty. I was hard to reach and had few friends, although there was one girl in my church who I secretly fancied. Too shy to approach her, I followed her home one day, hid in the bushes and peeked in her window. She saw someone in the bushes and called the police.

Imagine the shame I felt when my poor mother and grandmother had to come to the jail and bail me out. The charges were dropped as soon as the girl discovered who it was. But I was still required to meet with a social worker. Something in his eyes reassured me he'd been there. He knew suffering deep in his bones. He didn't just see the terror, shame or *nervousness* in me. He saw the good seed. It was a strange and amazing experience, to have a man encourage me to talk about my feelings. I knew instantly that I'd one day come to do exactly what he did. I'd see the good seed in everyone I met. I'd look straight into their eyes, and let them know with my whole heart, that they were okay, exactly how they were, no matter what they felt, what they looked like, or where they came from.

My Gift to You

I come to celebrate your *Humanity*, to remind you of your innate goodness, and to reassure you that there is no feeling in you that is inherently wrong. Or bad. No matter what you've done or experienced in life, you are innocent at your core. What matters now is not what you feel, but what you do with your feelings. I ask you, please don't reject your feelings, or react to them. Simply acknowledge and embrace any emotional *turbulence* within you with *Compassion*. *Nervousness* is only a sign that you have some feelings that need to be seen and embraced. Do not run from your pain, for along with your pain comes a great deal of pleasure.

Questions for Contemplation

• Where are you avoiding *turbulence* or change in your life?
• Do you ever find it hard to relax, to let people in, or to fully welcome your sexuality?
• Do you tend to attract emotional *crises*?
• What feelings do you judge the most as being bad or shameful?
• Who are the people in your life who have been able to see your *Humanity*, even when you couldn't see it yourself? Keep a list of these people in your journal. If you don't have anyone in your life right now who can do this, it may be time to seek out some support.

EQUALITY

*From the point of view of the human heart,
all humanity is one family.*

Gift: Equality
Shadow: Weakness
Siddhi: Tenderness
Programming Partner: 40

~ Richard Rudd

MY WISDOM STORY

Though I was born into a girl's body, I always felt like a boy deep down. My family was conventional. My father worked; my mother took care of the children and was completely dependent on him financially. He often treated her disrespectfully and with *cruelty*, as if she were *weak, overly sentimental* and only nice to look at.

As I got older, I saw men like him ruling the world. So I rejected my father, the patriarchy, as well as the boy in me. In absolute solidarity with my mother, I would be a girl, no matter how painful or wrong it felt within. Without realizing it, I spent the following years using every 'masculine' muscle I had to idealize and fight for all things 'feminine.' I envisioned and worked for a world where women were the leaders. I became an activist and speaker, empowering women world-wide with my ideals. I also became financially independent and bartered with 'the big boys' for rights and privileges, on behalf of women everywhere.

Privately, though, I was an emotional wreck. I alienated my romantic partners constantly with unfair and *cruel* accusations and an insatiable need for emotional processing. The truth was that deep down I was fighting for one thing: acceptance. But I couldn't even give that to myself. I was too *weak* to share, much less own, how I felt inside, or how I wanted to live my life. I had zero trust that my romantic partners would still love me as a man. No trust that the world would ever accept a freak like me. I was convinced that if my feminist community discovered how I really felt inside, they'd no longer see me as a leader, but as an outsider, maybe even an enemy.

When the pain of hiding from myself was too great, I decided to drive to a transgender support group, in a town where I'd never be recognized. I sat in the back of the room, and just listened. My own story was told, over and over again, by different people. Because of their courage, I found myself: my pain, longing, loneliness… and overwhelming fear. At the end of the meeting, someone came up to me. To my shock, it was someone I knew. I expected an attack, but instead, I was given the most tender embrace. In that moment, I knew I'd find my way back to me, and that I wouldn't have to do it alone.

My Gift to You

I am your friend. I have deep respect for you. I don't want you to change who you are at your core. You are a completely unique, worthy being, and there is a place for you in this world of ours. I see you with deep *Tenderness*. It is time to take your place, with pride, humility and profound self-acceptance. When you look at yourself, see your *weakness* and vulnerability as your strengths. When you look out at the world, see beyond polarities, beyond gender stereotypes, beyond patriarchy and matriarchy. Aim your eye towards synthesis, to the entire continuum of beauty available to all of us. *Equality* is your birthright. You and me, we are family.

QUESTIONS FOR CONTEMPLATION

- Is there a part of yourself that you've been refusing to love? How can you best accept and support your whole self right now?
- What do you see as a *weakness* in you? Can you find its inherent strength?
- Can you embrace all people equally? In what situations do you find this challenging?
- If you could show yourself *Tenderness* today, what would you do?
- Share your *Tenderness* with someone who could truly use it.

PERSEVERANCE

Over time, through perseverance, love and trust, you will eventually attain victory and experience your own divinity.

Gift: Perseverance
Shadow: Struggle
Siddhi: Honor
Programming Partner: 39

~ Richard Rudd

38

MY WISDOM STORY

My older brother died when I was just a child. My mother went into a deep depression. As a boy of action, I fought with all of my might to pull her out of her grief. But her pain consumed her, until she ended her own life. Her act of utter *defeat* was unthinkable in our land. I heard people talking, and it made me so angry my whole body shook.

Not knowing what to do with the overwhelming tension I felt, I started fighting wherever and whenever I could feel my impact. I loved the feeling of exerting my body. Fighting (and winning) gave me a sense of purpose and power. But sometimes I took my *aggression* out on helpless animals and my younger siblings. I became addicted to the struggle, and rarely knew when to stop.

As I grew older, I became a powerful warrior, with a gift for inspiring others to act. But my personal feelings often clouded my judgment. Once I led a whole army to war because someone from another village insulted my mother's *honor*. Many people were injured, even killed, at my insistence.

Just before we launched another attack, a young boy from the warring village, the same age as my older brother when he died, ran up to me and flung his arms around my waist out of pure desperation. He pleaded with me to end the feud, crying, "Why are we fighting? I don't understand!" As his question penetrated my deaf ears and hardened heart, I woke up.

I started breathing again. I hadn't even realized just how tight my chest had been, for years. He was right. I knew in that moment, that if my mother were alive, she would never want me to kill innocent people to defend her *honor*. There was already more than enough suffering and struggle in our village. And there I was, her son, fighting for everything that didn't matter. I wasn't *honoring* anyone. That's when I realized that deep down, I'd come to believe that if I had nothing to fight, I'd disappear, just like my mother did. Just like my brother. Everything changed after that. I took that sweet boy under my wings, and now we only fight for causes that are worth fighting for—those that are for the good of all people and the earth.

MY GIFT TO YOU

I am here to call out the sacred warrior in you. It's time to *Persevere*, to be the heroic underdog. Do not give up the struggle. Just be sure that you're fighting the right fight. Obstacles are a natural part of life. They are here to test your commitment, hone your abilities, increase your aliveness and unleash your life purpose. It is time to embrace your *defeats*. Let them make you stronger, more resilient and supple. You have the potential to turn a battle into a dance, to empower the people you love to liberate themselves from victimization. When you fight for love, not fear, everyone wins. There is no need to overthink or worry about appearing foolish. Now go find a cause you can pour your whole heart, body and soul into.

QUESTIONS FOR CONTEMPLATION

- Where in life are you fighting yourself? Does self-blame or a strong inner critic often leave you disempowered and depleted?
- Are you afraid of fighting, even for a worthy cause?
- Do you tend to fight the wrong things and the wrong people?
- Does a combative style sometimes sabotage your relationships?
- What is a cause worth fighting for?
- Think of a time you *Persevered* and you were glad you did. How did the experience feel? What did it require of you?
- Take a stand for something or someone today. *Honor* what truly matters.

DYNAMISM

If you do what you truly love you will unleash your creative dynamism, and the more creative you are the more energy becomes available to you.

Gift: Dynamism
Shadow: Provocation
Siddhi: Liberation
Programming Partner: 38

~ Richard Rudd

MY WISDOM STORY

Everyone called my father a Saint. At church, he was a dynamic and passionate preacher. At home, he was strict, mean and *provocative*. We weren't allowed to play like the other kids. We had to study scripture and help around the church. If we misbehaved or acted childishly, he threatened us with fiery damnation. He knew just what to say to instill the fear of God in us, and just how to say it.

While my siblings nodded 'yes, sir,' disappearing into passivity, frozenness and fatigue, I felt *trapped* and got angry. I had a mouth on me, too, and constantly called out his hypocrisy. Once I yelled, "You're no Saint! Having you as a father is Hell!" My words got him so mad he struck me with a belt. Afterwards, instead of apologizing, he said he only wanted to keep me out of trouble, and from being damned. But I didn't buy his excuses.

When I left home, I promised I'd never be anything like him. As I became a man, I used the sharpness of my tongue to criticize his religion, to defend my choices, the way I lived and loved. For years, though we never saw each other, I was wrapped up in a massive power struggle with my father. Then came the call. My father was dying. It was time to say my goodbyes. I walked into his bedroom, and there he was, so small and helpless, and not at all the man I'd been so busy fighting. Unable to speak, he looked up at me and smiled.

For the first time in my life, I saw the child in him that was never allowed to play. I saw his love, his sorrow for how he'd treated me, his desire to keep me safe from the pain he'd experienced. I was overcome with love for the man. For the next miraculous 39 days, I never left his side. I read stories to him, played games with him and sang songs to him. And we laughed. When I sang his favorite gospel song, one I hardly knew I remembered, he drifted off peacefully to sleep.

The day my father died was the day I welcomed back the fire of creativity and passion into my soul. Today I am a preacher, with the blessed job of instilling in people—not the Fear of God—the Love of God. In my church, all are welcome. Heaven is experienced right here on earth. My father's Spirit speaks straight out from my heart, and together our words set people free.

My Gift to You

I come to tell you that it doesn't matter how bad your upbringing was. All unhealthy conditioning can be reversed. You can contribute to the field of violence in our world by *provoking* others, or allowing yourself to be *provoked*. Or you can explore your passions and unleash your *Dynamism* (your Genius) by simply letting yourself be, and play. Remember, Genius isn't unusual. It has nothing to do with knowledge, or with the mind. It arises the moment you allow yourself to do what you love. It is time for you to allow your horizons—and breath—to expand. If you *provoke* anything in the people around you, may it be their creative spark and a deep sense of *Liberation*.

QUESTIONS FOR CONTEMPLATION

- Where do you feel *trapped* or imprisoned by fear in your life?
- When you were a young child, were you allowed to enjoy and express your *Dynamism* and vitality, or taught to subdue it?
- Does your anger ever get the better of you? Do people sometimes feel *provoked* by you, and you don't always understand why?
- When was the last time you tasted true *Liberation*?
- Think of something that you loved to do or play when you were a child (7 and under). Spend some time engaging in that activity today. Notice how it feels.

RESOLVE

The 40th Gift of Resolve is about becoming adept at
giving to yourself. Ultimately, it is about
deep physical relaxation.

Gift: Resolve
Shadow: Exhaustion
Siddhi: Divine Will
Programming Partner: 37

~ Richard Rudd

My Wisdom Story

I was born into a family with spiritual and artistic traditions that went back thousands of years. But as a boy, I was stolen from my parents and forced into slavery. My master had nothing but *contempt* for me. He saw and treated me like an animal. I survived by giving of myself tirelessly, without complaint. When beaten for not working hard enough, I worked harder.

Because of my obedience and unusual strength, I was given increasing amounts of responsibility, thus stress. Eventually, my stomach started to burn, and my digestive system shut down. I got so sick and *exhausted* my master no longer had use for me. He threw me out, with nothing but the scars on my back.

A young woman found me in the dirt. She was dark-skinned like me, but she was free. She gave me shelter, nursed me back to health and found work for me. I didn't mind the low pay or invisibility. I *acquiesced* in my role willingly—grateful not to be beaten. For many years I worked very hard. But I was lonely, broken and deeply afraid of people. I only drew comfort from carving statues out of wood, like the ones my grandfather made before I was taken away. One day the woman saw my carvings and was impressed. She encouraged me to set up shop for myself. I said 'no,' but she was stubborn and intuitive.

The next thing I knew she purchased a small shop and hung up a sign with my name on the door. For the first time in my life, I was my own boss. This realization brought forth an ache so vast that I cried myself to sleep for a year.

As I embraced my pain, I grew to love what I did. It was hard work, but it didn't feel like it. My shop thrived, my stomach healed and my body grew young again. Eventually I let the woman into my heart, and she became my wife. It took us ten years to save up enough money to return to our homeland and start a new life.

The moment my foot stepped on African soil, I looked up at the open sky, inhaled the sweet air, and my entire being relaxed. Then I heard the distant sounds of my people singing and drumming, waiting for us to join them. I looked into the eyes of my beloved, and knew I was home.

My Gift to You

I come when it is time to relax, and for you to understand the importance of balancing your desire to serve the world and your need to enjoy your life. Do not be afraid to stand your ground, set healthy boundaries or be generous with yourself. Your time and energy are precious. Sometimes saying 'no' to the right thing can be more powerful than saying 'yes.' I'm not asking that you rest now and then. I want you to relax, deeply and fully, with your whole being. When you are genuinely relaxed, you are free to work in harmony with your true nature and environment, and will have all of the energy required to complete any task, no matter how great. The health of our communities and nations depend on people who have true inner *Resolve* and a balanced physical, emotional and spiritual life.

QUESTIONS FOR CONTEMPLATION

- Where (with whom) do you find it most difficult to set a limit? What are you afraid of?
- Where are you not valuing yourself and your precious energy?
- What (or who) in your life exhausts you?
- Have you learned how to enjoy your solitude?
- Are you getting enough alone time? What truly relaxes you?
- Do you keep others at a distance because of painful experiences?
- Have you ever felt your inner *Resolve* aligned with *Divine Will?*
- Allow yourself to say 'no' to someone or something today. Write your reflections in your journal.

Anticipation

Genius manifests whilst non-genius dreams.

Gift: Anticipation
Shadow: Fantasy
Siddhi: Emanation
Programming Partner: 31

~ Richard Rudd

My Wisdom Story

I grew up in an impoverished and drought-stricken village. My parents owned a small farm and were able to provide the villagers eggs, milk and a listening ear. As a young child, I heard countless stories of people living lives of quiet desperation.

While most young girls dreamed of marrying and having children, I closed my eyes and imagined myself a Priestess of the Great Temple—laying my hands upon the sick, using my psychic abilities to reunite people with their destinies, and bringing fertility back to the land. But then I opened my *dreamy* eyes and felt overcome with heaviness.

For years I tried to fill my mind with visions of a glorious future in order to keep the pain of the world away. I drove myself relentlessly with my unrealistic *fantasies*, reading every book I could find on healing modalities and sacred plants. I even sneaked into a forbidden library to learn about ancient ceremonies where initiates entered sacred bridal chambers and left their bodies, to return again, awake.

While my sisters became wives and mothers, I became a *hyperactive* bundle of nerves. I disregarded my body's signs of fatigue and pushed on, until I could barely eat, much less study. I lost my strength, as well as my faith in the impossible and isolated path I'd chosen.

To make things worse, my mother fell ill from having cared for me for so long. One day, to our family's shock, a Priestess from the Great Temple knocked on our door. She was a magnificent, radiant being, who was told during a meditation to travel to our home, on foot. She floated her hand above my mother's chest, and I watched in awe as the spark in my mother's eyes returned.

In that moment, it dawned on me that in all the years I had spent filling my mind with knowledge, I had never dared to apply it. I was too terrified to try, and to fail. A wave of shame came over me as I realized how powerless I was to help my own mother. As if she could hear me think, the Priestess pierced into my eyes and soul, and said, "Dear child, you cannot do this work with your mind. Nor can you do this alone." Then she took my hand and said, "I came for your mother. But I also came for you." That day marked the beginning of my true apprenticeship and life's work.

MY GIFT TO YOU

I come when it is time for a new experience. A new world or life chapter is beckoning you. Every cell in your body is intricately linked, just as every impulse within you is communicating to the whole of creation. If you listen carefully, you can *anticipate* what is coming, as well as what is truly needed. You hold the key to your dreams in your own hand, and it is your responsibility to turn that key. But remember, you are not here to manifest your dreams on your own. Allow others to participate. And take one small step at a time. Pace yourself. Ask for help. Rest when you need it. Don't over-do or under-do. Do not expect things to turn out exactly as you imagine. Then embrace the thrill of *Anticipation*.

QUESTIONS FOR CONTEMPLATION

- Where in your life do you tend to feel 'too full'? Or 'too empty'? Do you tend to go back and forth between the two?
- Do you *fantasize* a lot, but have difficulty making things happen?
- Are you so driven to manifest your dreams that you burn out?
- Track your thoughts in your journal today: How much time did you spend obsessing about the future? Or rehashing the past?
- Share a dream with someone you trust. Let them in. Let them influence the shape and direction of your dream.

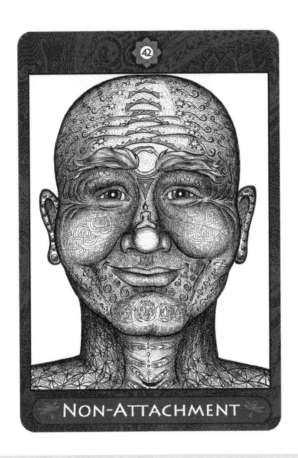

NON-ATTACHMENT

Detachment represents the process of letting go of control over your life, physically, mentally and emotionally.

Gift: Detachment
Shadow: Expectation
Siddhi: Celebration
Programming Partner: 32

~ Richard Rudd

MY WISDOM STORY

Known as the eternal optimist, I was always on my way towards something. The fulfilling relationship. The exciting job. The radiant health. I knew, once I achieved that perfect life, I'd be able to rest and be happy. So I rushed past every milestone, always *grasping* and *expecting*, always willing to put off my enjoyment in the NOW for a better future moment.

As I got older, I began to obsess about time. There was so much to do, and it felt like time was running out. Until it did. During a basic medical check-up, something unexpected was found. I was diagnosed with a deadly illness.

Suddenly, my life was spinning out of control. I was terrified, enraged. "I have no time for this!" I screamed inside, secretly feeling I'd failed at life. My optimism vanished, along with my faith in myself and others. For the next few years, I exhausted all of my savings, as well as my loved ones, as I leapt from doctor to doctor, from conventional to alternative treatments. Terrified nothing would work, I abandoned each treatment before it had a chance to succeed. My practitioners saw me as *flaky*. But all I saw was disappointment, and the slow death of my dreams.

Finally, I became so ill that I was hospitalized. There was no spark left in me, until I met my roommate, a child who was dying, too. Her spirit was so full of joy and wisdom that my heart melted. She called me her Buddy, and shared about her own impending death with an acceptance and peace that put me to shame.

The day she died, my heart literally stopped beating. The doctors tried to revive me, while I floated up and out of my body and was drawn into a tunnel of indescribable light, color and music. I felt a Love beyond anything I'd ever known. Then I saw her, my friend from the hospital, skipping through a field of flowers and into my arms. Elated, I scooped her up as she whispered, "It's time to go back, Buddy. There's still so much to *celebrate*." The next thing I knew I was back in my body, feeling calm and full of gratitude, despite the pain.

That was many years ago, when I first became known as a medical miracle. Now, when people look into my eyes, they feel my trust in life. I am not afraid—for myself, or for them. I've made peace with death. Now I am free to live, love and appreciate each moment for the precious gift it is.

MY GIFT TO YOU

I bring to you the Gift of *Non-Attachment*. I'm here to remind you that everything in life must come to an end, so that something new can be born. It is time to surrender to your life, and accept your death. This does not mean you stop desiring, caring or feeling.

In fact, I want you to feel—and breathe—even more intensely than you ever have. Nor does this mean you can't hold *expectations.* Just hold them lightly, without attachment. Trust the intelligence of your life, with its ebbs and flows, joys and pains. Even the most sorrowful states can be enjoyed if you can let your attachments fall away. Remember, you are an unfolding tale, its author and reader, all at once. Never miss an opportunity to *celebrate* your magnificent self, and life.

QUESTIONS FOR CONTEMPLATION

- Where are you resisting change? (e.g., the aging of your body, the individuation of your children, an old way of thinking or being)
- What is coming to an end, or needing to die in your life?
- What—or who—do you need to let go of?
- Have you prematurely abandoned a project, relationship or experience? What would it take for you to have true closure?
- Embrace a change in your life. Find a concrete and empowering way to *celebrate* it.

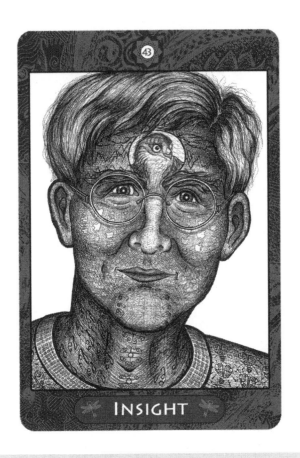

INSIGHT

Every human being is born to be a rebel in the sense of filling a space in the world that cannot be duplicated by another.

Gift: Insight
Shadow: Deafness
Siddhi: Epiphany
Programming Partner: 23

~ Richard Rudd

My Wisdom Story

I *worried* a lot as a kid. My mind spun with speculations about the bad things that could happen, and how I could avoid them. My more sturdy brothers teased me for being such an emotional wimp. At school I was called 'the brain.' I felt different and weird, and wanted so badly to fit in, to feel secure and be successful.

Ironically, my ability to anticipate problems made me a great programmer. No one could find and fix bugs like I could. Suddenly it was cool to be a nerd. As a young man, I had wealth and independence. Thrilled I could finally compete with my brothers, I dominated the conversation during family visits, talking endlessly about my successes at work. *Deaf* to their contributions, I showed off my latest gadgets, gave unasked for technological advice, and blurted out inappropriate comments about how big my abs were after hiring a personal trainer. I was too busy winning their approval to notice what a pain I was, or how deeply I envied their relationships.

Then I'd go home and pull out my feel-good technology. I'd play video games, watch TV and surf multiple dating sites at the same time. Obsessed with 'freeing up my time' to be more productive, I learned to operate my stereo, TV, computer, car, solar panels and sauna, all from my phone. But instead of freeing up my time, technology swallowed it whole. The harder I worked to streamline my life, the more complicated it became. I couldn't stop the *noise*.

That's when I had a breakthrough *Insight*. Nothing I did, used or accumulated would ever make me feel more comfortable in my own skin, or like I truly belonged in this world. In one fell swoop, I canceled all of my subscriptions and threw my TV and gadgets in the closet. And I got quiet. Really quiet.

All I did was listen—at first to the *noise* in my own head, then to the sounds of my home, then to the birds in my backyard. Slowly, I brought back technology. First the music, then the podcasts—touching ones with stories about real people who suffered and prevailed. That's when I received the *Insight* that would change the course of my life. I'd create a radio show for and in honor of the people who felt like me. I'd call it, "The Outcast." That was just the beginning.

My Gift to You

I am here to invite out the rebel in you—the poet, the lover, the mad scientist, the revolutionary. There is something only you can do. Something your entire life has prepared you for. It is time to take a risk, to shake up a system. You may make waves. That's okay. Whatever you do, stop listening to the status quo. This is not about venting or blaming; this is about being creative and being open to love. You don't have to know where exactly you're headed, or why, in order to trust your inner voice. As you courageously forge a new pathway, don't be surprised if your timing gets better and breakthrough *Insights* come your way. Dare to be who you are, and you will ignite the creative rebel in others, wherever you go.

QUESTIONS FOR CONTEMPLATION

- What are you *worried* most about these days?
- Do you obsess over your worries, or drown them out with busyness, outer *noise*, or your own talking?
- Do you ever feel misunderstood or like a misfit?
- How might your need to self-protect be deafening you to others?
- What might you do differently if you weren't afraid of being different?
- Have you ever had a deep *Insight* or *Epiphany*? What was it?
- Track your worry throughout the day. Watch it shapeshift.

TEAMWORK

The Gift of Teamwork is therefore about recognizing who belongs in your life.

Gift: Teamwork
Shadow: Interference
Siddhi: Synarchy
Programming Partner: 24

~ Richard Rudd

MY WISDOM STORY

My mother abandoned us when I was little. Though my father wanted to do right by his five children, he couldn't. He often got overwhelmed and disappeared for days, blowing his money on gambling and leaving me (the oldest) in charge of my younger siblings. I had no choice but to grow up fast and accept more responsibility than a boy should have to do.

As a young man, I wrote off all women, entered the work force, and naturally gravitated towards positions of leadership. People tended to trust me, and I preferred to be at the helm, even if it was the helm of a sinking ship. Time after time, no matter how good a job or organization looked on the outside, I managed to *misjudge* it. My higher-ups either disappeared or dropped the ball, my staff rarely knew what to do, and I'd be left picking up the slack.

Then I'd go through it all again somewhere else. I saw the same mess everywhere. In politics, in religion, in the economy. In love. Leaders were abandoning the people, and people were abandoning themselves and each other. And no one seemed to care. I *distrusted* everyone.

Until one day, a woman walked into my life that did care. Though she came from an indigenous background, completely different from my own, there was something strangely familiar about her. I liked her smell, and was immediately drawn into her world. She had an uncanny ability to trust—not just the trees, rivers and birds, but people. Me. She helped me see the perfect irony of my life, and how my childhood story was repeatedly *interfering* with my life, but in different disguises.

As soon as I saw the pattern, it began to change. My *distrustful* heart opened and for the first time in my life, I let a woman into my heart. As I surrendered to our intimacy, I developed quite a nose for people. More and more kindred spirits entered my life. Soon I was invited to work and live inside of a community that was capable of synchronistic and seamless forms of collaboration. I had never known this kind of joy or *Teamwork*. All participants contributed what they loved most; everyone shared the burden of responsibility. And much more often than not, things went smoothly. Now I know the true experience of belonging.

My Gift to You

I come to remind you that you always attract the relationships that teach you exactly what you need to know, in order to grow. The more you trust that people are in your life for a reason, the more you'll be able to learn the relational lessons you need to learn, and the better your judgment will be when it's time to choose new partners, friends and collaborators. I want you to trust your instincts. Start smelling the people in your life. Ask yourself, "Who are my true allies?" You have the potential to experience more trust, harmony and *Teamwork* in groups than you can possibly imagine. When you've found your true *team*, your destiny will naturally and magically unfold.

QUESTIONS FOR CONTEMPLATION

- Do you have difficulty trusting people? Do you keep them at arm's length?
- Do you keep running into the same unhealthy relational dynamics? Are your instincts often 'off'?
- What old relationships are *interfering* most with your new ones?
- Think of a time when you experienced or witnessed *Teamwork*.
- Draw a map of your current relationships. Indicate who are your true allies. Who do you trust? Who don't you trust? Be honest.
- Take a look at the people you've struggled with most in your life. If they were here to teach you something, what would it be?

Ultimately any system that has been built on a foundation of fear will by its very nature crumble.

Gift: Synergy
Shadow: Dominance
Siddhi: Communion
Programming Partner: 26

~ Richard Rudd

MY WISDOM STORY

I was born in a land where daughters didn't take over their father's empire. As a young girl, I was *timid*, but also caring and observant. I spent hours watching my father build the family business from scratch, working day and night, climbing up ladders and pleasing demanding investors. Once he achieved the power and authority he desired, he was determined not to lose it. He kept a tight rein on his employees, money, position and legacy. He never mixed business with friendship. Not even my mother knew the company secrets. As he aged, he grew increasingly paranoid, *pompous* and *dominant*. His temper was hot.

You can imagine the shock everyone felt when he left me in charge of the business after he died. My whole body quaked the day I was given the keys to the company safe. Most people expected me to fail, myself included. But my best friends believed in me, and promised their unconditional support.

The gratitude I felt gave me the courage to break the first rule of the family business. I invited my friends in. Instead of seeing them as threats, competitors, or needy parasites, I saw them as invaluable and trustworthy resources. I shared all that I knew, all that I needed, and then gave them the freedom to do what they were best at, without my interference.

At first, profits went down, and I worried that we'd go under. But the atmosphere of the company had changed. Goodwill, collaboration and creativity abounded. Soon our level of efficiency increased and profits rose. I invested most of our earnings into educating and training old and new employees in the fields of their heart's desire. Soon people stood in line, just for the opportunity to work for and with us. Over the years, our products and services became increasingly healthy for our customers and the environment. The life/work balance of our employees improved; their families flourished and even participated in the fun.

We became recognized and used as a model all over the world for our humanitarian efforts, capacity to share (as opposed to trade) resources, and our willingness to cross-pollinate with cutting edge businesses, non-profits, artists and activists. Not bad for a *timid* girl like me!

MY GIFT TO YOU

I am here to encourage you to take a leap and let go of your fears. Whether you are a member of a family, or a leader in a business, look for the ways that fear still rules your life. Where are you territorial? Where are you holding onto power that would be better shared? The time has come on our planet to begin organizing ourselves differently than we've done before. Competition is on its way out. *Synergistic* collaboration is on its way in. Though you may look at the world and understandably think that profitability is prevailing over goodwill, I come to reassure you that it isn't. Goodwill always wins in the end.

QUESTIONS FOR CONTEMPLATION

- Where are you too *timid* and afraid to rock the boat?
- Is it time to challenge an outer authority in your life?
- Where have you given into unhealthy competitive impulses?
- Where might you still be obsessed with climbing up a ladder?
- Think of a time when goodwill and collaboration paid off.
- Imagine participating in an exciting *Synergistic* collaboration. What kind of project would excite you most? Which of your gifts would you want to bring to the table? Who would you want to co-create with? If you don't know anyone specific, make people up! Journal the qualities you'd want your collaborators to have. Imagine your ideal creative *Communion*!

DELIGHT

Luck is what happens when you stop interfering with life.

Gift: Delight
Shadow: Seriousness
Siddhi: Ecstasy
Programming Partner: 25

~ Richard Rudd

MY WISDOM STORY

Though my parents wanted us to be happy, they were unhappy people. My mother was a *frigid* woman, ashamed of her body and obsessed with its every ache and pain. Terrified of evil spirits, she constantly reprimanded me and my brother when our play became too free or spontaneous. My father was a hard-working man with a traumatic past. Afraid our wild instincts would lead to danger, he tried to control our every move.

My brother reacted to our parents by taking nothing seriously, not even their punishments. He was always having fun, and they were always disapproving of his *frivolousness*. Once they had a fight that was so bad he stormed out of the house and never returned. Though I felt my parents' grief, I secretly envied my brother. Why couldn't I be laid back and free like him? Why did I have to care so much about what everyone thought? I was always wishing I was different—more clever, less fat, more successful.

As I matured, I came to understand that true happiness required more than physical beauty and outer achievements. So I prioritized the inner world and embarked on a *serious* spiritual journey. I sat in silence and prayed, participating in countless ceremonies. But still, I wasn't happy. I was still afraid of life, sure I was doing it all wrong, and that nothing would ever work out for me—not even enlightenment.

One day, as I sat under a tree struggling to meditate, an old woman appeared. She took a good look at me, my sacred altar and the somber expression on my face. Then, without asking for permission, she grabbed my hand and pulled me to a clearing in the forest by a beach. I'll never forget the sounds of laughter in the distance, or the glorious sight, upon our arrival, of the most gleeful gathering of women I'd ever seen.

In every shape, size and age, and dressed in the most fantastic clothing, they moved around a giant fire, singing and dancing with total abandon. Before I knew it, they took off their clothes and jumped gleefully into the water. I was laughing so hard I forgot all about how I looked, or what anyone thought. I threw off my clothes and twirled my way into the ocean. That full moon night marked the beginning of my Lucky life!

MY GIFT TO YOU

I come to share an ultimate truth: Nothing really matters but Life, and Love. It's time for you to enjoy life's small pleasures and to relax in your own body, no matter how it looks. You can surf life like an exciting wave, whether or not you understand what's happening. But to do this, you must first be willing to let go of the past, release all agendas, and keep your mind as open as your heart. Remember, the less *seriously* you take things, the easier it becomes to get out of your own way and allow life's *Delightful* surprises to take you exactly where you need to go, at exactly the right time. The magnificent and magical universe is at work in you, all of the time.

QUESTIONS FOR CONTEMPLATION

- Do you seem more laid back on the surface than you feel inside?
- Where are you taking life *too seriously*?
- Do you tend to worry about your appearance? Do these concerns ever keep you from enjoying your life, or taking risks?
- Have you ever experienced *Ecstasy*? Was it wonderful? Scary?
- Watch a funny, heart-warming movie. Smile.
- Pay attention to the little moments of *Delight* and signs of synchronicity in your life. Write them down in your journal.

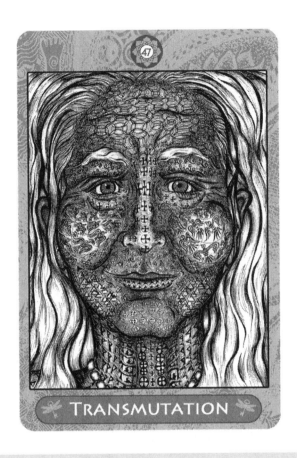

TRANSMUTATION

The only way to transcend suffering is to move more deeply into it, embracing every feeling and event that comes to you.

Gift: Transmutation
Shadow: Oppression
Siddhi: Transfiguration
Programming Partner: 22

~ Richard Rudd

47

MY WISDOM STORY

I had a recurring nightmare as a child. It always ended with a bearded man hovering over me with a giant blade, as I guarded something behind my back. I always woke up screaming, just before the blade touched my chest.

My father was a weak and quiet man. He didn't speak of his *oppressive* family past or believe in much of anything. My mother was a woman who religiously embraced the *dogma* of the church. Convinced a negative entity was attached to her daughter, she dragged me to church. For years, I prayed for forgiveness and to be rid of the evil, but the nightmare only intensified.

By the time I was a young woman, I avoided sleep at all costs. One night, I was so overcome with *hopelessness* that I broke down in front of my father, finally sharing the dream with him. He became strangely curious, as if he needed to know more. His surprising response awakened a curiosity—and courage—in me. That night, I willingly went to sleep. Though I still awoke before the knife fell, I was able to retrieve more information. The next night, the same happened. Then the next. It got to a point where I could enter the dream at will, like a sleuth, always leaving seconds before my murder. My father hungered for each new detail that came through. It was as if the two of us were assembling pieces from an ancient puzzle.

One night, I detected faint lettering on the bearded man's belt. I drew the three letters for my father. He ran to his room and rushed back with an old book full of Nordic symbols, given to him by the grandfather he'd never mentioned. Immediately, we saw the meaning of the three symbols: journey, gift and joy. I'd never seen my father's eyes glow like that. I couldn't wait to go to sleep that night. This time I let the dagger plunge into my heart. There was no blood, no pain. Just radiant light filling my chest. Turning to face what I'd been protecting all those years, I saw a treasure box, overflowing with jewels. The bearded man reappeared, this time beaming with kindness. Instead of a sword, he held a picture of my father as a child in his hand. He said, "Tell your father I ask for his forgiveness. Tell him I love him."

My father and I were never the same after that. Our ancestral relations strengthened, healed and transformed us. Today there is nothing I am not willing to see or feel. I uncover treasure after treasure.

MY GIFT TO YOU

I am here to ask you to move towards that which terrifies you. You may think you have a fixed identity, but you don't. You are forever changing. You are designed to bump up against limitations, and then to dissolve into something else. *Transmutation* is the key to your evolution. I come when it's time to hold nothing back, to embrace everything and to live dangerously. Release all definitions of who you are, or what you're capable of. Get comfortable with fear. Willingly take the lid off of Pandora's box. If you truly want to transcend your suffering, move deeply into it. Surrender. You can make a quantum leap at any moment, and your true purpose will be revealed.

QUESTIONS FOR CONTEMPLATION

- Have you given up on your life? Do you sometimes feel like no matter what you do, your life won't get better?
- What are the fears you refuse to face or deal with?
- Do you feel best when you're mentally certain about something?
- Do you ever feel *oppressed* by your own mind?
- Is it hard to relate to people who think differently than you?
- Think of something that truly scares you. Move towards it with a symbolic or creative act.
- Reflect on a time in your life you experienced a *Transmutation*.

RESOURCEFULNESS

If we don't know how to handle emotional states with equanimity, integrity and clarity, we never fully enter adulthood, but remain at some level children.

Gift: Resourcefulness
Shadow: Inadequacy
Siddhi: Wisdom
Programming Partner: 21

~ Richard Rudd

MY WISDOM STORY

My father was an idealistic young man who was willing to sacrifice his life for our country. He admired the bravery, cooperation and loyalty he experienced during the war, almost as much as he hated the way he and his fellow soldiers were received after it ended. He felt dropped and forgotten by the very people for whom he gave everything, and manipulated by the government he had served with such devotion.

By the time I was halfway through elementary school, he was a bitter, paranoid and *unscrupulous* man. When he wasn't obsessing over conspiracy theories and spying on the government, he was unleashing his anger at me, constantly criticizing me for being undisciplined and unattractive.

My mother was consumed with making ends meet, running the household and keeping up appearances. All she wanted was for me to do well in school and look good, so that the neighbors wouldn't notice what was happening behind closed doors. As my sense of unworthiness grew, I found myself glued to the television, watching soap operas filled with beautiful people, and commercials that flaunted perfect women who were gorgeous, successful and seductive all at once. In comparison, I felt unbearably *bland*.

As I entered puberty, the pressure I felt to look, act and perform well, increased. I became obsessed with my appearance, grades and getting into the best college. I couldn't sleep before tests. Desperate to fill the void in my belly and calm my nervous system, I binged and purged with food.

It wasn't until I was in high school, thanks to a wonderful English teacher who encouraged me to write about my most private pain, that I came to understand how my life had been hijacked by a deep sense of *inadequacy*. My teacher didn't just see my suffering; she saw a depth, sensitivity and *wisdom* in me I didn't even know was there. She kept pulling it out of me. I have her to thank for the way my life unfolded as I blossomed into a young woman, came to trust my inner knowing, and fell in love with earth-based spirituality.

Today I sleep peacefully and have the great honor of facilitating emotionally and spiritually healing rites of passage for 7 to 14 year-olds. Every day I am inspired and amazed by the inner resources of these kids.

MY GIFT TO YOU

Do not hide from the well of darkness within you, for there is light and boundless riches at the bottom of that well. You can find elegant solutions to all of life's challenges, and just the right support when you need it most. But first, you must reassure your body that it is safe, even when you don't have all of the answers. Let the parent in you love and hold the child within, even in the presence of fear. Over time, you will spontaneously dive into the void and discover more warmth there than you ever expected. Trust your inner knowing, and the people around you will start dipping into your well and drawing out more *Resourcefulness* and *Wisdom* than you realize you had. You are far more adequate than you can possibly imagine.

QUESTIONS FOR CONTEMPLATION

- What is your relationship to fear? Do you tend to repress and avoid your fear? Or do you tend to act it out, or react to it?
- Where do you feel most *inadequate*? How does 'not feeling good enough' impact your thoughts, feelings and actions?
- Do people tend to feel intimidated or inadequate around you?
- Who in your life has truly seen your *Wisdom* and pulled it out?
- Think of a time you experienced or expressed your *Wisdom*.
- Write down 10 of your greatest *inner Resources*. Notice the feelings and thoughts that arise as you do this.

REVOLUTION

As long as you see your own people as good and others as evil, you remain a prisoner of the 49th Shadow.

Gift: Revolution
Shadow: Reaction
Siddhi: Rebirth
Programming Partner: 4

~ Richard Rudd

My Wisdom Story

I was born a passionate, sensitive idealist. Though my family was relatively liberal, my parents were not passionate people. They'd ignore anything for the sake of harmony, which brought out the hypocrisy-detector in me. My mother identified as a feminist, but she still made herself small, and my father let her. My parents considered themselves open-minded, but I saw the look on their faces when I brought home romantic partners of a different race, ethnicity or gender than expected. Our neighborhood prided itself on its progressive politics, but it also subtly discouraged certain people from moving in, rationalized wars and dehumanized 'others.'

It was the *inertness* and denial that angered me most. Beneath the anger was hurt. How could they not see what I saw? Or feel what I felt? When I confronted my parents and they refused to own their biases, we'd have huge fights.

I went off to college. My mind spun and my heart broke as I learned about the plight of so many oppressed peoples. I seethed when I witnessed any kind of systemic marginalization or institutional oppression. For years, I hung out only with like-minded activists and judged my parents (and most people) for not 'getting it.'

The more staunchly I fought for peace, the more my personal life was rife with conflict. If I detected a drop of racist blood in my romantic partners, I'd drop them. It wasn't until my best friend divorced me, calling me 'the most *reactionary* person she'd ever met,' that I woke up. Losing her was devastating, but also a gift. All this time, as I divided up the world into good and ignorant and *rejected* people left and right, I was desperately trying to avoid being *rejected*. My fear of *rejection* had caused me to shut out so many people, just because their worldview was different than mine. It took time to move through the layers of humiliation, guilt and regret. Only when I was able to forgive myself could I begin to repair my personal relationships.

Finally I understood in my heart just how deep our human tendency is to split the world into black and white, us and them. This realization released a creativity in me I never knew was there. Now, instead of *rejecting* the old world, I channel all of my love and energy into envisioning and co-creating a new one. My approach to the peace movement has become delightfully peaceful.

My Gift to You

Welcome to the Peaceful *Revolution*. If you long to bring harmony to your community, begin by being patient, gentle and compassionate with yourself. Give your feelings time, space and plenty of creative outlets. But do not judge them, for when you do, you create an internal pressure that intensifies the feelings and the impulse to act them out. *Rejecting* yourself only makes it more difficult to see objectively, soften the heart, understand the other and see possibilities for resolution. If you must rebel, then rebel against your inner impulse to attack—anyone. When you resist the urge to react based on your emotions, or to be violent towards yourself, you are doing your part to end violence in the world. Be *revolutionary*, not *reactionary*.

QUESTIONS FOR CONTEMPLATION

- Do you prioritize harmony over aliveness, depth and honesty?
- Do you often push people away before they come too close?
- Do you *reject* people before they have the chance to *reject* you?
- The next time you feel emotionally triggered and are tempted to react, lash out or *reject* someone, ask yourself, "Am I feeling *rejected*? Am I afraid of being *rejected*?"
- What is the most loving *Revolutionary* act you can do today?

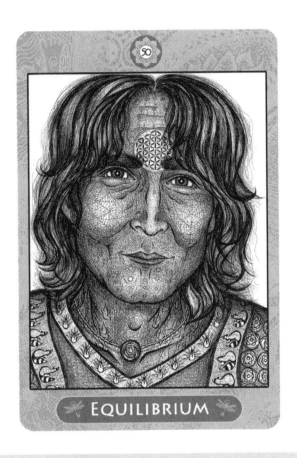

EQUILIBRIUM

Equilibrium can be lost,
but harmony is constant and infinite.

Gift: Equilibrium
Shadow: Corruption
Siddhi: Harmony
Programming Partner: 3

~ Richard Rudd

My Wisdom Story

Though my father wanted to be a musician and my mother a teacher, neither could afford the education. They spent their lives working in factories for little pay and for power-hungry bosses who only cared about the bottom line. *Overloaded* with responsibilities, my parents pushed their pain, shame and dreams away.

But I was angry—at their bosses, the industrialists, and all hierarchies. So I rebelled, and my parents worried about my angry outbursts at school. They feared my indignation would one day prevent me from earning a living. So they invested their minuscule savings to 'cure' me of what the schoolmaster called a 'mental illness.' But I knew I wasn't sick. Society was sick.

As soon as I was old enough, I grabbed my father's guitar and a philosophy book, and hitchhiked my way across Europe. Everywhere I went, I saw *corruption*. Wealthy people ruled the world, rich countries exploited the poor, and no one took responsibility for their destructive and dehumanizing impact. Most took credit for saving the world from chaos. Unable to contain my rage, I vandalized, then squatted in an abandoned building. When the police arrived, I refused to leave and was thrown into jail. Too ashamed to ask my parents to bail me out, I sat out the time. It was in jail that I realized just how *irresponsible* I'd been. Just like the capitalists, I hadn't held myself accountable for so many of my destructive actions. The selfish worldview that fed the hierarchies of the world was living in me.

I got brutally honest, faced my shame and fear, and came to understand just how much of my parents' pain I'd been carrying within me. As my heart broke open, my mind began to dream of a new world, where the self-actualizing needs of people like my parents were nourished and honored. As soon as I got out of jail, I was determined to get to know my parents in a whole new way. We even played music together. Then I started seeking out communities—even countries—that modeled new ways of organizing themselves.

One of the first things I noticed was how honest people were with each other, and themselves. I developed a special knack for spotting people's unlived dreams and encouraging them to take creative risks in honor of their gifts. I tend to have a strangely magical impact on any group I enter. Things often just fall into alignment, and I rarely know why.

MY GIFT TO YOU

I bring you a vision of a new world, where peace, *Harmony* and collaboration prevail. In you, I see a potential for inner peace, and a gift for bringing *Equilibrium* and balance to any group of which you're a part. To ignite these gifts, you must first be willing to put all of your hidden agendas on the table. Own and take responsibility for your ulterior motives, and your self-trust will grow. With self-trust, you can create the safe space necessary for others to face and embrace their own *Shadows*. This is how to co-create a truly peaceful world. There is a self-organizing intelligence that naturally arises when people are empowered to be who they are, and are encouraged to contribute passionately to the ever-evolving whole. Remember to be playful. What's the point of a new world if we can't enjoy it?

QUESTIONS FOR CONTEMPLATION

- Are you stuck working in—or against—'the system'?
- Is your social responsibility getting in the way of your creativity?
- Have you ever been blinded by power, or involved in *corruption*?
- Think of a time when you felt especially creative, playful or free. Where were you? What were you doing? Who were you with?
- What can you do to connect with an experience of *Harmony*?

INITIATIVE

Creative initiative is the path of every human spirit. Every one of us must at some point in life leave the crowd and head off into the uncharted wilderness of our heart.

Gift: Initiative
Shadow: Agitation
Siddhi: Awakening
Programming Partner: 57

~ Richard Rudd

MY WISDOM STORY

When I was just a toddler, several monks appeared at our door. After vigorous testing, I was recognized as the incarnation of a spiritual master. My parents were not religious people. They were shocked, but too subservient and *cowardly* to fight for me. I'll never forget crying as I was taken away from my mother.

For one year, I was bathed in love and attention by my appointed teacher. I loved him so much. He always showed me pictures of my parents, reminding me of our connection. But one day our monastery was brutally attacked by *hostile* soldiers who hated our people. My beloved teacher was killed.

Before I knew what had happened, I was swept up into the arms of another monk. We escaped through the mountains and arrived in another monastery. Though well cared for, I was terribly jumpy and nervous. I had trouble focusing on my studies. It was hard to trust anyone. My mind and heart understood I was safe, but my body didn't. It was always on guard and desperate to release its *agitation*.

Violence wasn't an option, so my mind took over. I became obsessed with moving up the ranks in the monastery, and constantly reminded myself that I was special because I was chosen so early. I was determined to be the first of my peers to *awaken*. To my peers, I seemed fearless, disciplined and precocious. But deep down, I was traumatized.

Thankfully, my new teacher saw the terror in me and understood the shock I'd been through. He also knew that shock would be one of my greatest teachers. One day it would help me release the false security of the ego, accept the certainty of death, and *awaken* to Oneness. But he also wisely knew I was too young to understand this. Instead of a lecture, he gave me a paintbrush, a canvas, and the freedom to do whatever I wanted.

His instruction was simple: "Follow your heart." The first stroke felt like jumping off a cliff. But soon I was filling the canvas with colors and symbols unlike anything seen before. My body relaxed, I made friends and lost interest in competition. At first I believed I was creating something new through the art. But now I know I am only rediscovering and retracing an eternal truth. There is no need to bring something new to the canvas, only to unveil the canvas itself.

MY GIFT TO YOU

I am not here to lead you; I am here to *Initiate* you. It is time to step off the beaten track, release everything you've ever been taught, and embrace an entirely new way of being. Though may stand upon the shoulders of others, in the end, only you can take the leap. There is no safety net. No way to avoid fear. If you want to transcend fear, move through it. Honor your creative impulses, wherever they take you. Let your awe-filled heart lead you back to your own heart. Good fortune is inevitable when you trust the love inside of you. If you do have a need to compete, do not compete with others. Funnel your competitive urges into your own creativity. And soon you will find competition replaced by deeply fulfilling collaboration.

QUESTIONS FOR CONTEMPLATION

- Do your fears keep you feeling *agitated*, hopeless or shut down?
- Do you shy away from life? Or do you engage in risky behaviors?
- Does your competitive drive get in the way of your relationships?
- Do you ever draw out the *hostility* in others, and not know why?
- Think of a time you faced a fear and experienced a breakthrough. What were you afraid of? What and who gave you courage?
- What leap are you being called to take at this time of your life? Find a creative way to explore an unknown.

RESTRAINT

The more selfless your intention,
the more power it will have.

Gift: Restraint
Shadow: Stress
Siddhi: Stillness
Programming Partner: 58

~ Richard Rudd

My Wisdom Story

As a young farm boy, I dreamed of a bigger life. I was a ravenous reader, and it didn't take long before I started writing myself. By some stroke of luck, in my early twenties, I wrote a fast-paced historical fiction novel that was discovered by a major publisher and raced straight to the top of the bestseller list. As soon as I received my first royalty check, I moved to the big city, where I was invited into a hip workspace full of cutting-edge writers. It was in that bustling space that I wrote my second novel.

To my dismay, it was a flop. My fans complained, my best critics wrote hurtful reviews, and my publishers threatened to pull my next contract unless I could guarantee another hit. As I faced my next project, I was paralyzed with fear. My hip workspace suddenly felt chaotic and noisy.

Stressed out and *stuck*, I spent hours staring at a blank screen, my mind racing with loads of self-doubt and no inspiration. I got so desperate, I started reading books about how to write bestsellers. Though I tried to follow the templates, nothing worked. My *restlessness* grew to the point where I couldn't sit still. Finally, exploding from the pressure, I kicked my desk, abandoned the building and my contract. I took the first flight out, and ended up on a small island, where I rented a tiny house in the country and spent months burned out and depressed.

At one point, I started gardening. For weeks, my hands were deep in the earth, and my mind's only concern was how to make plants grow. As my body and soul adjusted to a slower-paced life, I learned that, while I could enhance a plant's growth with gardening techniques, most of the time plants knew perfectly well how to grow. They had their own timing. I also noticed that when I was in a good mood while planting seeds, the plants seemed to do better.

Such small realizations reawakened the philosopher—and writer—in me. This time, I was inspired to write poems, each word like a flower. When I felt strong enough to go back to the big city and clean up my mess, I realized that the *stress* I'd felt there wasn't just mine. It was everywhere and everyone's. My heart went out to humanity, and I knew my next book would illuminate the impact of *stress* on all of us. My writing would serve the planet. This time I trusted the right words, and all of the inspiration I'd need, would come at just the right time.

My Gift to You

I come to relieve you of your *stress*, and to remind you that everything in nature (including you) has its own timing and growth pattern. Your intentions are like seeds. If you start something from a place of fear, the seed of fear will permeate the entire endeavor.

So if you want your dreams to grow and thrive, just hold a clear intention, infuse it with goodwill, and trust that your dreams know just how and when to bloom. It's time to befriend *Restraint*. Practice *patience*. Learn how not to interfere. Let your life and dreams unfold without too much pushing or prodding. And remember, more often than not, growth and transformation take place below ground, and the greatest seeds take the longest to germinate.

QUESTIONS FOR CONTEMPLATION

- Where are you feeling most *restless* and impatient?
- Where do you feel most *stuck*?
- What are the ways you experience (and express) *stress*?
- Is your body currently showing signs of burn out?
- Think of a time you practiced *Restraint,* and it paid off.
- Reflect upon a current project. How can you re-infuse it with goodwill and a loving intention?
- What is a simple way you can reconnect with *Stillness* today?

EXPANSION

True growth expands beyond its comfort zone—
it is continually transcending its last level.

Gift: Expansion
Shadow: Immaturity
Siddhi: Superabundance
Programming Partner: 54

~ Richard Rudd

My Wisdom Story

There was always balance and simplicity amongst my people. Nature provided us with what we needed, and we never took more. We each had our roles and contributed to the community. All of us prospered.

During the time of modernization, my family moved into an Arctic town to participate in contemporary life. My husband struggled to learn the language and ways of the new culture. He couldn't find work. I had a flair for language and took advantage of available educational programs. Soon I found a job in a weaving shop and became the primary wage earner for our family.

My husband fell into a deep depression. Alcohol made him *solemn*, controlling and abusive. He forbade me from trying new things and accused me of stealing his rightful place as head of the family. I felt frightened and trapped in my marriage. Driven to break free, I ran towards change. At first, I was *fickle*, hopping from opportunity to opportunity, and often dropping the ball.

But then I used my head, combining my traditional weaving skills and new training to launch my own clothing business. As I studied the modern world, my marketing improved and business grew. Soon I was able to leave my husband. Determined to remain independent, I read books about the fascination wealthy 'moderners' had for my people, our spiritual traditions and belief in reincarnation. I created a line of high-end sacred cloaks for affluent seekers. Blessed by Inuit shamans, they were to be used in meditation and during burials to enhance the soul's chance for a favorable incarnation.

The cloaks hit a chord in the market. My ambitions grew along with the size of my bank account, stress levels, and the complexity of my life. I expanded the line and started to mass-produce, using artificial materials and refusing to see how I was misusing sacred traditions and taking advantage of modern people's fear of death and longing for Spirit.

It wasn't until I visited one of our factories in China that I discovered how poorly our workers were treated, and how much garbage our factory produced. I was horrified to see how unfathomably far I'd drifted from my roots. I'd become a lonely, greedy and *immature* person. So I sold my business and donated my money and time to support disenfranchised indigenous peoples, integrate authentic wisdom into the world where Spirit was sorely missing, and restore the health of our home, the earth. My work is still expanding, but my life is simple and balanced. Finally I know what true prosperity is.

My Gift to You

I bring the Gift of *Expansion*. There is something in your life that you've outgrown. It's time to move beyond your comfort zone.

If you've been holding tightly to an opinion, identity, vision or worldview, it's time to let go. If you've been trying to reject a part of your past, or your life, assuming it has no gift for you, it is time to embrace it. Surrender your intellect, and watch everything become more simple and efficient. The mind has trouble understanding how everything is always passing away and beginning again. But the truth is that synthesis is happening all of the time; you are forever becoming whole. In the end, all that matters is *Expansion* through the heart.

QUESTIONS FOR CONTEMPLATION

- Do you sometimes feel overcome with sadness?
- Are you walling yourself off from the world and new experiences?
- Do you often begin things and never complete them?
- Have you outgrown a part of your life? Are you afraid to let go?
- Are you growing too fast, at the expense of your life balance?
- If you weren't afraid to expand, what might you expand into?

ASPIRATION

Greed is an energy that will compromise its own integrity in a flash to get what it wants, and this is its downfall.

Gift: Aspiration
Shadow: Greed
Siddhi: Ascension
Programming Partner: 53

~ Richard Rudd

MY WISDOM STORY

I grew up in the ashram of a charismatic guru. Following in the footsteps of my materially *unambitious* parents, I became a devotee. At a young age, I was adept at meditation and prayer, and knew the sweet scent of peace.

Our guru preached generosity and rejected all possessions. He was known for performing miracles and for his great humility. Once I got lost in the ashram and accidentally passed by one of his private chambers. The door was ajar, so I could peek in. I was shocked to see mountains of material riches and pictures of him socializing with some of the wealthiest, most corrupt people in the world. Before anyone saw me, I ran straight to my parents to tell them what I saw. They didn't believe me. Even if it were true, they were sure he had a holy reason.

For the next few years, my parents continued to offer their salaries and material goods to the ashram, and he continued to receive their gifts with his hidden *greed*. Finally I dared to confront him. He accused me of lying and sinning. My parents were too scared and confused to stand by my side.

So I ran away from the ashram and everything that guru represented. All I wanted was self-realization. I rejected all material goods and lived a completely ascetic life. For years I lived under a tree, then wandered for long periods, in total silence. People began to see me as a Saint. Though I resisted the projections for as long as I could, my yearning to serve grew too big to ignore.

I began to teach about love, forgiveness, service, charity, contentment, inner peace, devotion and respect for all peoples, no matter their caste or religion. I advised my followers to lead ordinary family lives, and not to give their resources to me. But then there was a devastating earthquake in our country. Thousands were left homeless. I realized that with one request, I could raise enough money to save all of those people.

In that moment, I understood how profoundly my fear of *greed* had diminished my capacity to serve. To heal the wounds of my past, I had to learn to trust myself, and to understand at the deepest level, that my hands were nothing but the hands of the world. Now I have a Foundation where resources are constantly gathered and redistributed. Food, money and love flow freely through my life, home and community. I hold onto very little, but I no longer need to push anything away.

MY GIFT TO YOU

I bring the Gift of *Aspiration*. Look long and hard at the ways you're still driven by fear, competition and the desire to serve yourself. I come when it is time to start thinking about how to serve others, and how to join forces in order to create a healthier, more sustainable world. Call out your inner Robin Hood. Start giving back. Think holistically. Find creative ways to more justly redistribute the resources on our planet. If you don't have money, donate time, energy, wisdom and love. Remember, if you've been holding onto what you've got, this is a good time to let it go. If you've been resisting others' generosity, it's a good time to receive. Keep it flowing and all will thrive.

QUESTIONS FOR CONTEMPLATION

- Where is your life flowing? Where are you holding back?
- Is your integrity being compromised by your ambition?
- Has the desire to own and accumulate taken over your life?
- Have you given up on your ambitions out of disillusionment?
- Is your rejection of materialism preventing you from receiving?
- How can you open up more to receiving?
- Take stock of what you have. Where is there excess? Find 3 things that you can give away or redistribute today.

FREEDOM

It is always at the very end, when we have all but given up hope of redemption that liberation comes.

Gift: Freedom
Shadow: Victimization
Siddhi: Freedom
Programming Partner: 59

~ Richard Rudd

MY WISDOM STORY

From as early as I can remember, I was moody. I constantly searched for outer reasons to explain my moods, and spent my entire youth chasing after everything and everyone I believed caused me joy, and avoiding or blaming those I held responsible for my pain. As I matured, instead of longing for superficial 'feel-good' opportunities, I yearned to feel personally free, romantically fulfilled and spiritually enlightened.

So I embarked on a quest for the perfect soul mate, teacher and heightened state of being. I became a professional seeker, tantric whiz and workshop junkie. I fell in and out of love with so many people, practices, and gurus I lost count. When I was in love, I believed I was free.

But actually I was trapped and addicted to the never-ending hope of romance, the dream of liberation, the catharsis of drama. I was hooked on disappointment, and how secretly great I felt complaining about my unending stream of bad luck. The rollercoaster had no end. My emotions ruled me. Even though I could see and explain all of 'my issues,' I was still hopelessly blind to the fact that I wasn't taking responsibility for my life. I was still giving my power away to something or someone 'out there,' who could rescue me, or make me miserable.

In the end, it was all about me. *My* love. *My* awakening. *My* happiness. *My* disappointment. It wasn't until I met a woman who saw into the core of my *victimization* that my heart cracked open. I could no longer hide from her, or myself.

It was through the intimacy of our relationship that I learned to face my deepest fears and most hidden agendas. For the first time in my life, I *rose in love* instead of falling. Not just with her, but with all of life. I stopped complaining and blaming others. No longer burdened by complicated stories and devastating dramas, I was free to feel much more deeply and fully, and to make decisions without agonizing and second-guessing. No longer clinging to teachers or techniques, I started experiencing the kinds of synchronicities I'd always dreamed of. Just naturally, I did more of what I loved, writing songs, enjoying friends and spending time in nature.

Now people tend to relax around me. They feel free to be who they are. I now know deep in my soul that I am connected to all of life.

MY GIFT TO YOU

I come to tell you that the *Freedom* you seek has nothing to do with what you do, what you understand or how you feel. It has to do with the attitude you embrace, no matter what is happening within or around you. Can you live your life without over-relying on outer paths, systems and structures to keep you safe? Can you fully feel whatever you're feeling, without getting lost in drama or the stories of the mind? Can you experience a longing, without rushing to meet it, or escape it? Can you find peace during painful moments? Can you embrace not knowing? Can you simply be? *Freedom* is yours the moment you give up the thought that someone else is responsible for your life, or that you are separate from life. Practice transparency and radical self-acceptance, and you will discover your magnificence.

QUESTIONS FOR CONTEMPLATION

- Where are you your own worst enemy?
- What and who do you tend to complain most about, or blame?
- Where do you most feel like a *victim*? Be honest.
- What systems or structures do you find yourself relying on, or hiding behind? What might happen if you let them go?
- Think of a time in your life you felt *Free* and empowered. How would you describe your overall attitude at the time?
- Go one day without complaining or blaming. See what happens.

56

ENRICHMENT

True enjoyment is rooted inside your being rather than in the external.

Gift: Enrichment
Shadow: Distraction
Siddhi: Intoxication
Programming Partner: 60

~ Richard Rudd

MY WISDOM STORY

I was a creative kid who hated school. My parents were too busy paying the bills and watching the news to notice how bored and trapped I felt (or how unhappy they were). As I entered my teens, I became *sullen*. I'd come home from school, shut the door and listen to hours of music, while numbing myself out with weed. I was either *distracted*, lost in fantasy, or blaming my parents and teachers for being so clueless and robotic.

When I turned 14, I got a guitar and became obsessed with writing and playing music. I wrote about everything I saw and felt, about the loneliness and emptiness in our busy world. Eventually I got up the courage to play my songs on the street. My music hit a chord with the young people. Soon I was discovered by a big record company and signed my first deal.

As a young man, I played concerts all over the country and lived the rock star life. I took as many lovers as I took drugs. My performances were deep, and my audiences were always moved. But I was too high to feel any of it. Over time, I needed more and more *stimulation* to feel anything. I couldn't get high or *overstimulated* enough, so I kept grasping for that next extreme experience, until I overdosed and almost died.

When I woke up in the hospital, all alone, I realized just how out of control and empty my life had become. There was no balance. No love. No genuine connection. I'd become just like the busy lonely people I wrote songs about. And I realized that, if I truly wanted to uncover the richness of life, it could never come from the outside. I had to go within, and feel. So I did. I went cold turkey on all of my addictions. For a while I thought I'd die from the physical discomfort. Once I made it through the withdrawal, I realized that the real challenge was facing and feeling all of the emotional pain I'd been avoiding for so many years.

It took a long time for me to learn how to live a truly balanced life. Today, a single song can move me to tears. A drop of wine is enough to relax me. And I just love hanging out with people, laughing and spreading the cheer.

MY GIFT TO YOU

I come to bring you true *Enrichment*, not mere enjoyment or entertainment. I want you to get the most out of your life, so that you can enhance the lives of others. But first you must learn to balance fun with seriousness. And you must wake up to all of the ways you *distract* yourself from who you are and how you truly feel. It's time to learn to discern between that which genuinely nourishes you, and that which saps your spirit. Notice where you are still a victim of your senses, of overindulgence and self-deprivation. I care less about what you do than where you come from. Come from fear, and you'll likely do too much, too little, or at the wrong time. Come from love, and you won't need rules and protocols to guide you. Eventually, your attention will turn inwards towards gratitude, and your presence will *enrich* the world.

QUESTIONS FOR CONTEMPLATION

- What or who are you unable to say 'no' to?
- Where do you overindulge? Where do you self-deprive?
- Do you sometimes feel sullen, numb, as if your spirit is depleted?
- Are you often overstimulated?
- What are your most powerful *distractions* these days?
- Think of what, and who, truly *enrich* your life.
- When was the last time you enriched someone's life?
- Pick a favorite *distraction*. Give it up for a day. See what happens.

INTUITION

Every time you trust in your intuition or make a decision based on it, you raise the frequency of your whole aura.

Gift: Intuition
Shadow: Unease
Siddhi: Clarity
Programming Partner: 51

~ Richard Rudd

My Wisdom Story

My mother had three miscarriages before I was born. During her pregnancy with me, she was anxious, and when I was young, she was a *hesitant*, overprotective mother, constantly worrying about my getting sick or into an accident. She clung to rationality as if her life depended on it. But her endless lists of pros and cons paralyzed her. They also made my father impatient and his actions *impetuous*, which usually resulted in financially risky decisions, and an even more anxious mother.

I was close to my parents and could sense their thoughts and feelings as if they were my own. As I matured, I saw how their ways of coping with life were causing them pain and frustration. When it came to decision-making, the opposing strategies of over-rationality and impulsivity seemed equally unhelpful. Longing to resolve their unrest, I sought alternative ways of accessing truth and knowing.

I became a student of *Intuition*, reading books on ESP, using oracle decks and training my psychic abilities. But when I discovered the deep, vast world of astrology, a light went on. I couldn't get enough. After obsessively studying natal charts, I learned about the world of transits, and my prayers were answered. Finally I had a way of reading the future and helping people cope with anxiety and life's uncertainties.

My career instantly took off, and eventually astrology took over my life. To do anything or guide anyone, I needed the stars' blessing. I became attached to the money, status and security brought by my success and, over time, I became increasingly paranoid and out of touch with my *Intuition*.

When I dismissed my own hunches about my beloved mother's health because the stars said otherwise, and she got sick, I was overwhelmed with shame and guilt. How could I have drifted so far from my own inner knowing? That's when it hit me. Life was uncertain. No matter how skilled I was, or how accurate astrology was, I could not control Life or rescue the people I loved from the unknown.

For five years, I didn't track a single transit. I learned to face and fully feel the pain, and beauty, of uncertainty. Now I use my *Intuition* and astrological tools from a place of love and playfulness, not fear. I am finally at *ease*.

MY GIFT TO YOU

I come to remind you of that still voice within that connects you to all of life. Your *Intuition* is one of your greatest gifts. Trust it. We live in a world that is obsessed with reason. There is so much emphasis on exploring and conquering the mind. But you have the ability to experience true knowing. You can perceive something even before it can be seen, heard, touched or tasted. It is time to embrace your primal instincts, and to stop relying on theories and methods. I am not suggesting you discard your intellect, or your tools. Only that you allow them to serve your *Intuition*. As you learn this art, you will find that old fears melt away, relationships soften and things go more smoothly. Trust the delicate hairs on the back of your neck. Listen carefully.

QUESTIONS FOR CONTEMPLATION

- Do you sometimes ignore your *Intuition*, or say 'yes' before you're ready, because you're afraid of missing out? Or because waiting for *clarity* makes you too *uneasy*?
- Do you miss out on wonderful opportunities because you are afraid of trusting your instincts and taking a leap?
- Do worries, doubts and anxiety make it hard to hear your *Intuition*?
- Pay special attention to that still small voice within, your clear, instantaneous knowing. What is it telling you right now? Follow it today, even if your mind is resisting. See what happens.

VITALITY

Increased vitality really means increased freedom.

Gift: Vitality
Shadow: Dissatisfaction
Siddhi: Bliss
Programming Partner: 52

~ Richard Rudd

MY WISDOM STORY

As soon as I could stand up, I was on a surfboard. As a young boy, all I wanted to do was play in the water and ride the waves. One day, while surfing, I experienced a moment of pure *Bliss*. I spent the next ten years trying to recreate that experience. I worked hard to improve my instincts, stamina and skills. The stronger I got, the more compelled I felt to improve the world as well.

So I dove into self-help philosophy like the ocean, swimming from book to book, and teacher to teacher, but never finding any that truly satisfied me. The only truths that really made sense were the ones I learned from surfing. Surfing taught me about healthy and unhealthy fear. It taught me about perfectionism and flexibility. It taught me about joy and freedom. It taught me about being in the Now. So I wrote a book about it, and before I knew it, I was on tour, inspiring people all over the country.

But still I felt *dissatisfied*. Teaching and traveling were stressing me out, and I wasn't surfing enough. So I booked a trip to a renowned surfing site, determined to unhook from the world and reconnect with my joy. But a wave came that I wasn't prepared for.

The damage to my body from the accident was so great that I was told I might never walk again. It was while lying flat on my back in the hospital, for months, that my true spiritual path began. At first, my spirit was crushed. But over time, as I accepted that this was my new life, I began to learn, at the deepest level, that there was no future, and no past. There was only Now. Any time I fought that truth, I was *interfering* with Life itself.

As I surrendered to this truth, I began to experience unexpected moments of *Bliss*, though I had very little to be happy about. Within two years, I was walking. Within two more, I was back on a surfboard. I was so grateful to be there at all, that all attachments fell away. It wasn't about the waves, my skill or performance, or even about how great the experience was. It was just about Being. A tiny drop, and the vast ocean, all at once.

Today I bring people of all shapes, ages and abilities to the ocean to swim with the dolphins. Every day I witness waves of joy and freedom well up from within them. I do not regret one moment of the painful yet transformative journey that brought me here.

MY GIFT TO YOU

I'm here to tell you it is time to stop fighting your true nature. You were born with a life force and *Vitality* within you that must be expressed. You can attempt to interfere with it by trying to recreate it, or by resisting *dissatisfaction*. But there's nothing you can do to get rid of the life pulsing within you. So you might as well surrender. Dissatisfaction is a natural part of life. Without it, none of us would evolve, or be motivated to make this world a better place. When you allow life to express itself through you, without resistance or judgment, *Bliss* happens naturally. The future is not in your hands; it does not even exist. All there is, is Now. So stop projecting into the future, let life have its way with you, and watch your purpose unfold.

QUESTIONS FOR CONTEMPLATION

- Are you still clinging to the belief that you can, and should, create a perfect, peaceful future that will last the rest of your life?
- Are you still trying to recreate an old experience of joy?
- Are you looking for happiness outside of yourself?
- How have your unsatisfying experiences contributed to your evolution and growth as a person? To the service you provide?
- When have you experienced your *Vitality*, or a moment of *Bliss*?
- Make a list of your life's greatest *Dissatisfactions*. How do you try to resolve or avoid these *Dissatisfactions*? For a day, or a week, go on a 'resolution/avoidance' diet.

INTIMACY

As this heart opening occurs, true intimacy is born and two people meet within a single awareness.

Gift: Intimacy
Shadow: Dishonesty
Siddhi: Transparency
Programming Partner: 55

~ Richard Rudd

My Wisdom Story

My parents had a strong chemistry, but their relationship was fraught with tension and conflict. My father constantly complained about being trapped. When he went out at night, my mother would bombard him with *intrusive* questions and throw fits when he wouldn't fess up to his latest extramarital escapade. Usually he'd go off in a huff, removing himself from family activities. But instead of sharing how excluded he felt, the whole fiasco would repeat itself.

Throughout my childhood, my parents kept so many secrets and never came clean with their hurts. I was a deep, shy and introverted teen. Unlike my siblings, I could never figure out how to interact with the opposite sex. It all seemed so messy. So I stayed home while my siblings dated, and felt excluded like my mother. Even when they invited me along, or tried to set me up, I was convinced they just pitied me and didn't want me there, so I refused.

As I got older, I developed friendships with men, but was never attracted to the nice ones. When with someone I felt attracted to, usually a bad boy, I'd feel a surge of mistrust and shut down. Until I met a man I couldn't resist. Our sexual chemistry was so powerful it felt spiritual. For the first time, I *fantasized* about marriage and children.

He wasn't a bad man, and I sincerely believe he cared about me. But I couldn't control my fears, or their control over me. To avoid losing him, I hid aspects of who I was and played games to keep him interested. I often doubted why he wanted to be with me, so I excluded myself from his social life, and then felt rejected. Or, when I felt him slipping away, I'd try to prevent him from having a social life. When he called me controlling, jealous and *dishonest*, I broke up with him.

It took me a long time to grieve the loss of that relationship, and to feel the terror beneath the sadness and anger that I'd been carrying with me since childhood. That was the beginning of a long journey towards radical honesty with myself, and in my relationships. Today, my beloved partner and I counsel couples, helping them own their fears, share their truth, open their ears and their hearts to each other, without pulling or pushing away. *Intimacy* is my greatest teacher, and my spiritual path.

MY GIFT TO YOU

It's time to come clean with the people you love. To be truly Intimate, you must be totally honest with yourself, and be willing to accept and express your deepest fears. Understand, when you open a door to another person, you are letting go of control and opening yourself up to being influenced on a deep emotional level. If you carry wounds from the past, as most of us do, this can be scary.

Whether you fear being trapped or abandoned, do not judge your feelings. You will be rewarded with unleashed creativity, beauty and sensuality, and the wonderful possibility of communing with another human being, in one field of awareness. There's no limit to what two open hearts can do together.

QUESTIONS FOR CONTEMPLATION

- Is your fear of being abandoned by a romantic partner keeping you from being honest? From committing more fully? Is it causing you to over-seduce or try to control your partner?
- Is your fear of being trapped sabotaging a current (or potential) relationship? Are you often planning your escape?
- Do you sometimes feel *excluded,* or *exclude* yourself out of fear?
- Are you often puzzled by the people you are attracted to?
- Think of a time when you were courageously *Transparent.* How were you received? How did you feel?
- Journal and reflect upon your biggest 'relational edges' when it comes to trusting others. How can you stretch yourself?

REALISM

The only thing needed for magic to occur is some form of a structure and an open mind!

Gift: Realism
Shadow: Limitation
Siddhi: Justice
Programming Partner: 56

~ Richard Rudd

My Wisdom Story

I grew up in a part of the world where religious fanaticism, poverty and *injustice* were the norm. In response to oppression, people prayed for miracles. As a child, I also prayed—for a better world where women and children were given more rights.

But as I got older, I grew tired of praying. Magical thinking wasn't doing anyone any good, and I didn't trust my country's laws, or its lawmakers. When the dictatorship was overthrown, it became possible for girls like me to go to University. Immediately, I knew I would become a lawyer, so I could change our country's sick system from the inside.

The only girl in my entire family to ever receive a higher education, I buried myself in studies, learned every law imaginable, and became a skilled debater, backing up every argument against the current oppressive system with irrefutable evidence. My work life was successful, but inside I was lost, *unstructured*, and my relational life was non-existent. I had no true allies. My mind had become closed, limited and *rigid*. I had forgotten how to dream, and had lost touch with the love of *Justice* that drove me to learn and serve.

I even started resenting the very women whose rights I'd been fighting for. If they didn't agree with me, or appreciate all that I was doing, I'd fly into a rage. I found them completely oblivious to what it actually took to make their dreams of a better life a reality. But they were angry with me because I was so busy protecting their rights that I stopped loving, respecting and regarding them as human beings with their own voices.

When one of my most loyal supporters returned to her fanatical roots, I woke up, stopped arguing and started listening to the actual dreams, needs and desires of the people I represented. Now I see beyond the surface of things, and honor the oppressed part of everyone. I use my understanding of the law to support and empower. My open mind and dreaming heart inspire all that I do. I've learned that true *Justice* takes a village, and that changing the world for the better can actually be an enjoyable, relationally nourishing process.

MY GIFT TO YOU

I bring to you a love of *Realism* and common sense. I want you to stay connected to your ideals and visions, without losing sight of the practical aspects of the creative process. Just as a seed needs a shell, and a river needs its banks, your dreams need you to understand the inherent structures of the world, so that you can bring them to life. Do not see these structures as stifling or forever-lasting *limitations*, but as supportive vessels, perfectly designed to take you where you need to go, and no further. Remember to keep the heart of your dreams close, while holding all systems, religions and mindsets lightly. Get comfortable with uncertainty, think outside the box and use playful language. Seeming plateaus don't mean nothing is happening. Everything of true value lives within you. So be the eyes, ears and mind of our Universe, and soon you will be making magic!

Questions for Contemplation

- Do you tend to run away from structure and commitment?
- Have you had trouble finding true allies?
- Are you rarely involved in something that lasts?
- Do you hold on tightly to your own way of thinking and doing?
- Without certain structures in your life, would you fall part?
- If you tend to be too limited: Pick a structure you hold *rigidly* and find a concrete way to hold it just a tad more lightly this week.
- If you tend to be *unstructured*: Pick an area where you struggle with discipline, and experiment with following through.
- Reflect on your most positive experiences of *Realism* and *Justice*.

INSPIRATION

Creativity is the single most important Gift for drawing humanity out of its mass psychosis.

Gift: Inspiration
Shadow: Psychosis
Siddhi: Sanctity
Programming Partner: 62

~ Richard Rudd

My Wisdom Story

I was born asking 'why.' Why were boys more valuable than girls? Why was there war? Was God a loving God? I pondered these questions during a time in my country when they were forbidden. Though I learned to keep quiet, my fascination with religion continued throughout my young adulthood. Against the will of my religiously *disenchanted* parents and the *fanatically* atheist party ruling the country, I collected every bit of information I could from my older relatives, about Confucianism, Taoism and Buddhism.

When the new constitution passed and 'normal religious activities' were allowed, I immediately explored Islam and Christianity. When I moved to the West, finally free to explore anything I liked, I became consumed with the study of religions, especially those that had been forbidden to me.

The more I learned, the more complex the picture became. I had to know where did these religions, myths and archetypes originate in the first place? Why were there so many unexplained parallels between the world religions, going back thousands of years? Where (and from whom) did the impossible sacred monuments and temples truly come from? I turned to archeology, and was catapulted down a wormhole that challenged everything I knew about reality.

My journey took me from the Bible, to Egypt, to Sumeria, to Lemuria, to Atlantis, and farther. I uncovered so many holes in scientific thought that I had to consider the strangest possibilities, from ancient astronauts to stargates, rainbow bodies, time travel, multidimensionality, supernovas, orbs, giants and fairies. I became obsessed with reincarnation, the paranormal, UFOs, crop circles, and Near Death Experiences. Every new answer birthed a new question. People either thought I was crazy for believing certain things, or for not embracing their beliefs.

The pressure to understand the nature of reality became unbearable. When I finally stopped trying to get rid of the pressure, and instead stepped right into it, my intellect shattered. Even I believed I was crazy. But soon I realized that most people on the planet were basically *psychotic*. None of us saw reality as it actually was. In that moment, I stopped asking 'why' and was graced with true *Inspiration*. The most spectacular art began to flow through me. I no longer need to understand reality; only to experience it directly.

MY GIFT TO YOU

I come to say that you cannot force or predict *Inspiration*. The Muse appears on her own terms, in her own timing. She enters your life as a pressure, beckoning you into the unknown, calling you inwards and back to your origins. She is not always about fun and games. Sometimes she comes to dismantle your way of thinking, and to shake up your entire grasp of reality and your ability to love. To welcome her into your life, you must practice immense patience and trust. Be willing to receive your inner secrets, truth and the mystery that is all around you. Even when you can't feel her, know that she is working behind the scenes. Don't look for Spirit outside of yourself. BE Spirit.

QUESTIONS FOR CONTEMPLATION

- Might your certainty about a philosophy, system or path be hiding a deeper fear of the unknown?
- Is it hard to relax when you can't find the answer to a big 'why'? Try spending a period of time without working hard to understand.
- Have you given up on discovering who you truly are, and where you come from? Are you afraid of digging too deep? Pick an unusual inquiry for yourself, and go digging.
- Have you ever experienced a breakdown (physical, emotional, mental or spiritual) that became an *Inspiring* breakthrough?

Intelligence is of the heart, whereas intellect is of the mind.

Gift: Precision
Shadow: Intellect
Siddhi: Impeccability
Programming Partner: 61

~ Richard Rudd

MY WISDOM STORY

I was a vibrant child, always doing cartwheels and dancing with the wind. But in school, I was taught to sit still, learn the facts, and prove my *intellect* by doing well on tests and writing convincing essays. I was smart, so my brain quickly filled up with facts. The people around me expected me to become something important, so I fulfilled their expectations.

I went through medical school, where I learned about the human body, and just about every symptom, illness and medication. Before long, I was working long hours in a busy, prestigious hospital. When with patients, I looked for problems, took meticulous notes and ran their symptoms through my perfectly internalized lists of pathologies. I rarely sat down to look in their eyes, hear their stories or acknowledge their wisdom. I talked *pedantically* to patients who mentioned alternative healing modalities or the power of prayer. My behaviors were *obsessive*, and I was constantly avoiding my patients' pain, as well as my own.

It wasn't until an unusual patient entered my life that everything changed. Despite her own illness and suffering, she managed to see right past the stress I felt, and straight into the loneliness. In the middle of an appointment, she asked me how I was doing. Was I happy? Was there anything she could do for me?

For some reason, I opened up to her and shared about my life, the constant migraines, the feeling like I was drowning in a sea of details and responsibilities. At the end of our talk, she held my hands and calmly suggested I go to a yoga class. There was a teacher she wanted me to experience. For some reason, I listened.

I'll never forget how awkward I felt at the beginning of that class, or how my body and mind melted like butter with each pose, as I stretched, breathed and relaxed. The teacher moved with such ease, grace and *Impeccability*. Instead of speaking, she gently placed her hand on the small of my back, and tears began to flow. How I'd missed that cartwheeling girl who knew nothing about the human body other than how to be in and enjoy it. Now I integrate yoga, movement and meditation into everything I do. Even in the busiest places, my mind remains delightfully still. I listen more than speak when with patients, and am astounded by how much their own bodies know what they need. My heart and body are at peace.

My Gift to You

I want you to know the difference between the *Intellect* and true intelligence. The *Intellect* is your mind's ability to think, gather facts and manipulate knowledge through language. It is wonderful but limited. The more *intellectual* you are, the less true Intelligence you use. The next time you look around you, look with your whole heart. Take in the essence of our mysterious world deep into your soul, and you will begin to taste true intelligence. From this place, you will care less about potential humiliation, and more about speaking, writing and inventing with love. In the language of simplicity, you will become an embodiment of *Precision* and transform the world.

QUESTIONS FOR CONTEMPLATION

- Do you feel stuck in life's details, with no creative outlet?
- Is it hard to switch off your mind? Is it always going?
- Does your mind often pick apart the flaws in peoples' thinking?
- Go on a 'heart walk.' Instead of looking out at the world and noticing the facts, see if you can *impeccably* feel the spirit. Listen to the trees. Feel into the people. Notice how this experience impacts the way you feel and communicate. Be open to surprise, as you reconnect with your true *Intelligence*.

INQUIRY

The human logical mind is simply not designed to be certain of anything other than paradox!

Gift: Inquiry
Shadow: Doubt
Siddhi: Truth
Programming Partner: 64

~ Richard Rudd

My Wisdom Story

As a kid, I'd ask my parents a question, and they'd answer me with logic and certainty. Rainbows were meteorological phenomena, and unicorns were a physical impossibility. But there were still so many things I wondered about. The more my family laughed at my 'ridiculous' questions, the more I thought I was stupid.

As a young man, every thought, fantasy and opinion that occurred to me was poured through an internalized critical filter. I constantly doubted who I was, what I thought, what I did, how I felt. And I second-guessed every decision I made, either to a point of paralysis, or regrettable impulsivity. I couldn't relax until I got to the bottom of things, saw an entire pattern, or landed on an objective truth, which of course I could never find, which made me even more anxious.

So I learned more, and more... and kept my *self-doubts* to myself. Though agreeable and reasonable in public, I was angry and antagonistic in my intimate relationships. My lover would express a feeling, and I'd be so obsessed with locating the objective truth of the matter that I'd miss the point entirely. I became increasingly *suspicious*, always expecting others to disagree, doubt or misunderstand me. I picked fights, got defensive and gathered evidence, especially when they failed to get the complexity of a situation. Though I clung to the thought that someone had to be right, and someone else had to be wrong, it was never that simple.

When my *self-doubt* got so big that I could no longer sleep or function, I sought out professional help. For the first time in my life, I could openly share about the doubts that plagued me. At first I doubted the counselor could help me, but she hung in there, encouraging me not to act on my doubts, especially when they were at their most intense.

Over time, she helped me appreciate my mind's unique gift for *Inquiry*, and to embrace the paradoxical nature of Life. With support, I developed a mindfulness practice. As my mind became a more loving witness, I saw just how many people suffered from *self-doubt*, and how my struggles to understand were a part of what made me human. Now I help others experience various states of awareness and explore the mystery of their true nature.

MY GIFT TO YOU

I come to celebrate your love of *Inquiry*, but also to remind you that your inquisitive mind and gift for doubting are best used in service of the world, not in service of beating yourself up. See if you can remain genuinely curious about life, without insisting on finding answers. Stay open to learning as your understanding of life becomes increasingly complex and paradoxical. Be curious about your own suffering, for it will open your compassionate heart. One day your brilliant mind will lead you back to yourself. And how could it not? You are forever intertwined with everything you've ever learned.

QUESTIONS FOR CONTEMPLATION

- Are you plagued with *self-doubt*? Do your *self-doubts* make you anxious, or keep you awake at night?
- Do you tend to feel *suspicious* of the people in your life, of their motives and agendas? Do your *suspicions* tend to cause others to be defensive around you?
- How could your gift of *Inquiry* be used as a service in the world? Where has it already come in handy?
- What does *Truth* mean to you? How has your relationship to *Truth* changed over the years?
- Try doubting your *self-doubt* for a day. Notice what happens, and journal your thoughts.

IMAGINATION

If you allow your pain, or the world pain, to be expressed through an artistic process, you will see alchemy in progress.

Gift: Imagination
Shadow: Confusion
Siddhi: Illumination
Programming Partner: 63

~ Richard Rudd

MY WISDOM STORY

My grandparents suffered unspeakable cruelty during the war. They managed to escape with my parents, just before the rest of their family was brutally killed. They never spoke of what happened, and my parents knew not to ask. Instead of looking back, my parents devoted their lives to providing their children a safe and secure future, free of persecution, by focusing on our successful assimilation and keeping our family's pain snugly under the rug.

As a young girl, I wanted to please them, so I did my best to *imitate* those around me and kept my questions about our family's past to myself. But I felt out of place, like something essential was 'off.' To the outside world, my family seemed perfect. But at home, it felt like living with a herd of elephants in the room. I often felt *confused* and uneasy, figuring I was just too sensitive, intense and weird.

When the pain of not knowing where we came from got too great, I became determined to solve the mystery. I secretly studied all there was to know about the country my grandparents came from and my family's own tragic history in the war. Finally it made sense—the sheep-like behavior, the stubborn evasiveness about the past. At first my revelations lessened my *confusion* and increased my compassion towards my parents. But when they still refused to talk about any of it, I became angry with them for refusing to deal with their pain or talk about anything that actually mattered. I was tired of being repressed by their repression.

One day, when I couldn't take it any more, I cruelly accused my parents of cowardice, and then I flaunted graphic pictures from their past in front of them. Suddenly, in the midst of my outburst, my father clutched his chest in pain. Though he survived the heart attack, I was devastated and unable to forgive myself. Racked with guilt, I found a counselor who specialized in healing the wounds of history. With his support, I learned how, through my relentless attempts to end the *confusion*, I was avoiding my own pain, just like my family. So I let my mind go blank and my heart feel the pure suffering of my people.

That's when the miracles started, and my *Imagination* was unleashed. Now my life is a work of art, and everything I do is infused with the kind of light that can only emerge through darkness.

MY GIFT TO YOU

I come to set your *Imagination* free. But first, you must bless your pain and *confusion* with the gift of your awareness. In the presence of *confusion*, there is nothing to do. Nowhere to go. Nothing to figure out. *Confusion* is a totally natural human state. It is actually *holy ground*. So taste it. Embrace it. But do not try to change, interpret or get rid of it. As soon as you remember that you are not your *confusion*, its true diamond nature will emerge from the coal. And your *Imagination* will be released, so that you can give expression to your pain and inner demons through a fulfilling process of creativity. Whether you're expressing with a paintbrush or a pen, be honest, courageous, illogical and wild. Go where no one else has gone before.

QUESTIONS FOR CONTEMPLATION

• What are the ways you avoid feeling pain and *confusion*? By fitting in? Overthinking? Keeping busy? Getting angry?

• Where are you still hiding your originality?

• How do your current relationships reinforce your hiding?

• Think of a time when you made room for your *Imagination*.

• At this moment, what causes you the most pain or *confusion*? Find a way to express your pain, fear or *confusion* creatively. Don't make it great art. Make it honest.

The Mirror Card!

Be yourself; no base imitator of another, but your best self.
There is something that you can do better than any other.
Listen to the inward voice and bravely obey that.

~ Ralph Waldo Emerson, *Self-Reliance*

YOUR GIFT TO YOU

How wonderful you picked this card! Now you can look at your own beautiful, unique face and receive a wonderful gift from yourself. There are questions for you below. Be open to the possibility that each time you pick this card, or it chooses you, the answers that arise will be different. And why shouldn't they be? You are a forever-evolving mystery, a *Wisdom Keeper* in progress! Enjoy your own company.

And remember, you are a Gift to yourself, and to this world.

QUESTIONS FOR CONTEMPLATION

- What would you say is your greatest *Gift*, at this moment in your life?

- What fear do you struggle with most? How does it impact the way you think? Feel? Act?

- How does your fear keep you from exploring, embracing and expressing your *Gift*?

- Think of a time in your life when you felt filled with Spirit. Or emptied of your small self. Where were you? Who were you with? How can you reconnect with that experience now?

- Look in the mirror. Keep looking into your eyes. Notice the thoughts that waft through.

Do you find your mind making judgments?
Getting distracted? Asking questions?
Do strong feelings come up?
Allow for them if you can.
Do you feel nothing? Allow for that, too.
Whatever you're noticing, whatever is happening, embrace it.

Let it ... let you... be okay.

YOUR WISDOM STORY

Tell your own story in your journal. (Feel free to add to it over time!) Include struggles. Include significant relationships and turning points. Share the moments in your story when Fear won. When Love won. Where are you in the story now? Are you at the beginning, the middle, moving towards the end? Are you at a crossroads? Is this a turning point? What is winning in the story right now? Fear or Love? Doubt or Trust? Is there a simple thing you can do right now, or just accept, that might actually change the storyline completely?

You are the Gift!

CARD SPREADS AND SUGGESTIONS FOR THEIR USE

There are infinite ways to work with the *Wisdom Keepers*. Enjoy the following spreads, and feel free to come up with your own ideas, too.

Simple things to keep in mind:

Whenever shuffling or pulling a card, hold a question and intention in your heart. Ask for the right *Wisdom Keeper* to come to you, and that he or she serves your highest good. Consider using your non-dominant hand to pull the cards, to evoke the intuitive wisdom of your inner child, and help you release the mind.

Remember, it is impossible to make a mistake or receive the wrong *Wisdom Keeper*. Trust in the power of synchronicity, and engage sincerely and creatively in the process of contemplation.

Keep your questions clear yet open-ended, as opposed to yes/no questions. Keep them practical and grounded in the Now.

(This oracle deck is not intended to be used as a predictive device.)

1. Spread for Establishing an Intentional Relationship with a *Wisdom Keeper*

There may be times in your life where you feel a strong desire or need for the presence of a particular *Wisdom Keeper*. Or you may want to choose a card for a meaningful event or life cycle. For instance, you may want to choose a *Wisdom Keeper* each birthday, or on full moons, or special anniversaries. Trust what feels right. What matters here is that you look at all of the *Wisdom Keepers*, and that you make an intentional choice. Be open to surprise.

Questions to help you choose a *Wisdom Keeper* to focus on for a period of time:

Who is your *Wisdom Keeper*?

Who inspires you?

Who believes in you?

Who trusts you?

Who understands you?

Who sees into the eyes of your soul?

Who reminds you of something important?

Who would you feel safe confiding in?

Whose presence would feel supportive at this point in your journey?

Who recognizes your unique *Gifts*?

2. *Wisdom Keeper* Tonglen

Tonglen is a meditation method that utilizes the breath for the purpose of awakening passion, softening the heart, and overcoming the fear of suffering (our own or others). Usually, on the in-breath, we take into our own bodies the pain or fear of the 'other,' whether it be a particular person or the world. And on the out-breath, we send back love, relaxation or peace to the other, or whatever we sense would relieve their pain.

In this case, I invite you to sit with your *Wisdom Keeper*. Look into his or her eyes (or face). Then imagine that the two of you are simultaneously practicing Tonglen with each other. Each of you is breathing in the other's pain, and breathing out loving-kindness. Do this for 3 to 5 minutes, and see how you feel afterwards.

3. Spread for Daily Guidance and Contemplation

Choosing a *Wisdom Keeper* each day can be a wonderful way to focus your energies and receive support.

Shuffle and cut the cards in a way that feels right. Then spread the cards out, face down. Hold an intention in your heart that the *Wisdom Keeper* you need most right now appears. If you're moved to ask a question, do so. Then pick the card that 'lights up' for you.

4. Life Flower Spread
(B.L.O.S.S.O.M.)

Think of your life as a flower with many petals. This flower is holographic, in the sense that the health of each petal has a direct impact on the health of the whole flower. Allow the *Wisdom Keepers* to help your Life Flower Blossom, by bringing wisdom into each of the main areas of your life.

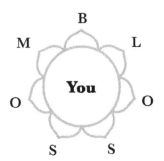

Choose a *Wisdom Keeper* for each of the following petals:

B (to support your **B**ody)

L (to reflect the **L**ove of friends, family and community)

O (to illuminate your relationship to a significant **O**ther)

S (to support your **S**pirituality)

S (to support your **S**uccess)

O (to reflect your relationship to the **O**rdinary aspects of life)

M (to support your deeper **M**ission)

You (to reflect where you find yourself today and what kind of support you could use the most right now)

(Feel free to add or make changes to the petals.)

5. Relationship Spread

This simple spread can support you in better understanding or enhancing an outer, or inner, relationship. Whether exploring a friendship, love relationship, work partnership or your relationship to your own inner child, be sure to stay connected to your heart when pulling each card, even if the relationship is feeling difficult right now. Feel free to ask a guiding question at the onset of this spread.

Pull three *Wisdom Keepers* for:

You (the *Gift* and *Shadow* you are currently bringing to the relationship)

The Other (the *Gift* and *Shadow* the other is bringing to the relationship)

Your Shared Journey (what the two of you are here to learn through your relationship, and the kind of support your relationship needs the most)

6. Family (or Group) Spread

Here you have the opportunity to explore the healing/learning potential of any group you're a part of, whether it is your family, work team, support group or spiritual community. Again, as you pick each card, make sure that you bring each person in the group into focus. Hold a loving intention, so that the *Wisdom Keepers* can shed light on the group's deeper purpose, as well as the *Gifts* and *Shadows* brought by each member.

**Pull a card for each group member,
including yourself.**

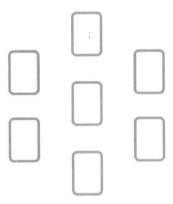

Place the *Wisdom Keepers* in a circle. Then choose one card to place in the middle to illuminate the deeper purpose and potential of the whole group.

7. Genealogy Spread

A Genealogy Spread can provide you with a profound understanding of the origins of your *Gifts*, *Shadows* and core wounds. By exploring such a spread, you can activate healing in your own life, and on behalf of your ancestors.

**Begin by choosing a card for yourself,
and then lay out a family tree of *Wisdom Keepers*.**

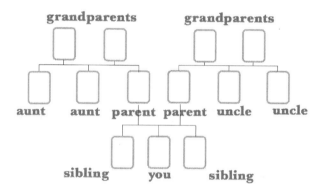

Let the cards represent the *Gift* and *Shadow* contributions of each of the relatives you've chosen to include in this spread (e.g., children, siblings, parents, grandparents, etc.). Hold each family member in your heart before pulling each card. A sincere exploration of this spread may take time and space. *Wisdom Keepers* can shed light on relatives you know well, open doors to family secrets, and help you understand your own strengths and struggles with a whole new perspective.

8. Creative Dream Spread

Think of a dream that you hold in your heart (e.g., to start or complete a project, find the love of your life, fulfill a creative passion, be healthier in your body, conquer a fear or travel the world). **Connect deeply with your wish before choosing 3 _Wisdom Keepers_ to shed light on:**

- **Your Dream**
- **What's in the Way** of your fulfilling this dream
- **A Focal Point** as you move towards the dream

9. Specific Challenge Spread

This spread is designed to help you work with a particular challenge. **Bring the challenge you're facing to your heart, then choose 4 _Wisdom Keepers_ to shed light on:**

- **The Challenge** you currently face (e.g. relational, health, financial, work, creative)
- **Your Desired Outcome**
- **The Shadow** that needs attention
- **The Gift** that will help you

10. Integrity Spread

Choose 4 *Wisdom Keepers* to help you cultivate the qualities that are essential to Integrity.

- One for **Courage**
- One for **Healthy Boundaries**
- One for **Kindness**
- One for **Wisdom**

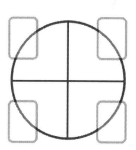

11. 9-Centered Chakra Spread

Choose 9 *Wisdom Keepers* to bring support and insight to each of the 9 Chakras of the body.

(inspired by Integral Human Design)

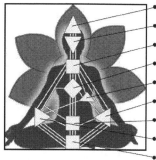

- **Head** (Inspiration, Knowing)
- **Ajna** (Mind, Thinking)
- **Throat** (Expression, Transforming)
- **Identity** (Self, Being, Loving)
- **Ego** (Will, Working)
- **Solar Plexus** (Emotion, Yearning)
- **Sacral** (Energy, Flowing)
- **Spleen** (Intuition, Sensing)
- **Root** (Impulse, Growing)

EXPLORING YOUR UNIQUE DESIGN THROUGH THE GENE KEYS

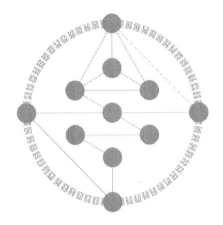

There are many ways to integrate the *Wisdom Keepers* into a deeper exploration of the *Gene Keys*, and your own very unique journey or 'Profile' (based on your birthday). There are three specific sequences that together make up the Golden Path. The first is called *The Activation Sequence*, which includes your *Life's Work*, *Evolution*, *Purpose* and *Radiance*. The second is called *The Venus Sequence*, which is deeply centered on Love, Relationship, and your development throughout the first 21 years of your life. The third is called *The Pearl Sequence*, which illuminates your relationship to prosperity, and guides you towards your most fulfilling role in, and contribution to, the world. (I'm sure there are more sequences to come!)

(Wisdom Keeper Spreads can be made for all of the above sequences.)

RESOURCES FOR GOING DEEPER

To learn more about **The Wisdom Keepers Oracle Deck,**
The Wisdom Keepers Inner Guidebook, and ways
to further explore **The Gene Keys Golden Path**: WisdomKeepers.net

To learn more about
The 64 Faces of Awakening Coloring Book:
64Faces.com/coloring-book.html

To learn more about the global outreach of
The 64 Faces of Awakening:
64faces.org

To learn more about the **64 Faces of Awakening** and
ways to purchase *Wisdom Keeper* art prints,
wall hangings and custom drawings:
64Faces.com

To learn more about **Rosy Aronson's work** with the
expressive arts, coaching and counseling:
RosyAronson.com

FINAL NOTE:
UNDERSTANDING THE COLOR CODE

As you'll notice, certain *Wisdom Keepers* share a 'color.' This is intentional, in that they belong to the same soul group, or what Richard Rudd calls the *21 Codon Rings* in the *Gene Keys*. Below I've described which *Wisdom Keepers* are associated with the same Codon Rings or soul family. For more information, refer to *The Gene Keys* book.

- The Ring of Fire (1, 14)
- The Ring of Water (2, 8)
- The Ring of Life and Death (3, 20, 23, 24, 27, 42)
- The Ring of Union (4, 7, 29, 59)

- The Ring of Light (5, 9, 11, 26)
- The Ring of Alchemy (6, 40, 47, 64)
- The Ring of Humanity (10, 17, 21, 25, 38, 51)
- The Ring of Trials (12, 33, 56)
- The Ring of Purification (13, 30)
- The Ring of Seeking (15, 39, 52, 53, 54, 58)
- The Ring of Prosperity (16, 45)
- The Ring of Matter (18, 46, 48, 57)
- The Ring of Gaia (19, 60, 61)
- The Ring of Illusion (28, 32)
- The Ring of No Return (31, 62)
- The Ring of Destiny (34, 43)
- The Ring of Miracles (35)
- The Ring of Divinity (36, 37, 22, 63)
- The Ring of Origin (41)
- The Ring of The Illuminati (44, 50)
- The Ring of The Whirlwind (49, 55)

CONCLUSION

I hope that this *Inner Guidebook* has provided you with inspiring ways to work with the *Wisdom Keeper*s. Most of all, I hope that in the years to come, you spend time with these beings. Look into their eyes, and allow them to see into you. Engage your full heart. And as you connect with them, may you ultimately discover that you are, and have always been, the *Wisdom Keeper* you are looking for.

A Special Acknowledgement

I simply must give a special acknowledgement to Ann Cameron of AC Creative, who stepped in when I needed it most, spearheaded and lovingly shaped the paperback edition of the **Wisdom Keepers Inner Guidebook**, and devoted more time, skill, wisdom, stamina and support in helping me birth all aspects of this evolving labor of love into the world than I ever thought possible from a human being. She is my creative partner and the brilliant driving force behind **64faces.org**. She is an editor, spiritual coach, publishing genius, marketing and public relations whiz, intuitive advisor, and one of the most talented writers I've ever met. She volunteered to help me when she could have been busy writing one of her many bestsellers-in-the-works (keep an eye out for her work, you won't be sorry!). And she did this out of the pure goodness of her heart, and an unwavering belief in the transformative powers of the **64 Faces of Awakening**. Some people go the extra mile. Ann goes the extra triathlon. To Ann, I say, from the bottom of my heart... Thank you!

WWW.AC-CREATIV.COM

About the Artist/Author

Rosy Aronson, Ph.D., is an Artist, Blossoming Guide and Authenticity Coach with a Masters in Expressive Arts Therapy and a Doctorate in Intuitive Listening & the Creative Arts. In addition to this *Inner Guidebook*, Rosy has created the *64 Faces of Awakening*, *The Wisdom Keepers Oracle Deck* and *The 64 Faces of Awakening Coloring Book* to reflect essential healing archetypes that lie at the foundation of our universe. Her deepest intention is to provide empowering tools for people to awaken to their gifts and bloom into their authentic selves.

An avid permission-giver, pressure-dissolver and embracer of the unknown, Rosy believes we are literally designed to blossom, and the more each of us radically trusts, honors and expresses our true nature, the more magic we can create together. Rosy holds the vision that over time, the *64 Faces of Awakening* will be invited into homes, retreat centers, public buildings, meditation halls, yoga studios and schools, so that more and more people can bask in the warm presence and compassion of these wise beings.